1+1=1

Kay K. Arvin

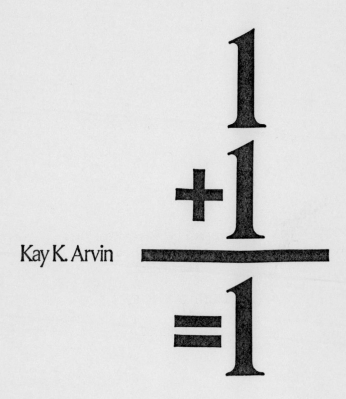

BROADMAN PRESS
Nashville, Tennessee

ISBN: 0–8054–8305–5

4283–05

Dewey Decimal Classification Number 301:426
Library of Congress catalog card number: 69–14364
Printed in the United States of America
2.5ML71KSP

To Les, the 1 who is the + of my equation
and without whom all the answers would be 0.

CONTENTS

1+1=1

1 The Reasons Why

The agreement of a man and a woman to become one—to combine their time, energy, money, their dreams, bodies, and personalities into one mutual effort—is entered into with a simple, "I do." This is the only simple thing about it. The perplexities of the union appear almost immediately and frequently become more and more compounded with the passing of time.

It is seldom that one finds a periodical for general public consumption which does not include some work on the subject of marriage, covering every possible facet of the whole idea of matrimony and all resulting situations. In fact, the need for coping with these situations has become so universal that an entire new profession has sprung up in an attempt to meet it. There are specialists in helping people understand themselves and others, specialists in finding means to peaceful cohabitation with one another.

The public, driven by tremendous need and impelled by longed-for hope, has tucked its pride under its arm and has formed waiting lines at the doors of these specialists. We are, after all, members of a nation of specialists and have reason for confidence. Opportunists, charlatans, semiskilled and highly skilled have all opened their doors to people's problems.

There has developed a good deal of class consciousness in it all, with each group a little inclined to disassociate with the other. This has been going on enough years now that lines of demarkation have begun to appear rather clearly so that most areas are well posted. What has become evident, as a result, is that the solving of problems is something of a problem in itself. Attitudes have jelled and time has passed sufficiently to allow the outlines of the marriage counseling picture to appear.

These outlines form a kind of iceberg-looking affair with two peaks projecting sharply above a great massive area which lies in between them. We will attach a flag to the top of each peak, labeling it "Area Helped." There are two because they each represent a different area. One is made up of families where the need for a psychiatrist has become apparent in one way or another. His analysis of the emotional problem of one individual reveals that the marriage relationship is responsible and, therefore, treatment must begin with, or must include, that relationship. It is quite difficult, after all, to divide life into unrelated departments which do not flow into and out of one another. The help offered here is of a professional quality with a price tag to match.

The other peak will represent an impressive number of persons who have received help with their marital problems through the facilities of governmental agencies. There are many kinds of these organizations, some based on ethnic groups, some limited to particular city or country boundaries, and some which have been organized to meet the needs of a specific religious denomination. We include here, also, the many marriages which have come under the supervision of the counseling services of the various types of family courts. These courts have been created specifically to help meet the overwhelming need for finding a way of handling the critical marital illnesses which, without remedial treatment, are certain to cause the marriage to expire.

The combined alleviated pain is incomprehensible and would have been suffered by the national community had it not been for the services of these places of refuge. Staffs are, for the most part, well qualified but almost always limited severely by serious personnel shortages.

Between these two identifiable groups lies the conglomerate of the many isolated situations which have come under the influence of some kind of counseling, either public or private. This includes the counsel of those specifically trained and also that of people whose advice is sought because of the special relationship which already exists, i.e. the minister, priest, rabbi, or the family doctor.

There is no real way of ascertaining the value and effectiveness of these hours of discussion and shared concern. Quite likely, however, only one partner of the ailing marriage participates, as the choice of consultant is made on the basis of the close relationship which exists. This fine rapport may not be experienced by the spouse. It is a safe assumption, though, that many, many homes are made happier because of the tensions and frustrations which have been eased as burdens have been taken from their secret hiding place, unwrapped, and laid bare for the patient scrutiny of another whose opinion is valued. While the professional know-how of counseling may be unfamiliar to these dedicated people, it may be more than compensated for, in a good many instances, by personal understanding and by that quality more precious than knowledge—wisdom.

This book is concerned with these people, those who have taken some small step, falteringly or bravely, toward a way out of their dilemma. It is concerned more, however, with the largest group of all. The group which does not appear on the supposed chart because of its elusiveness and its immensity. Alarm clocks ring every morning to rouse people to begin another day of a discouraged, colorless marriage or of a livid, deceitful one. Here and there, on a certain winter day called Christmas, or a sunny vacation, the birth of a child, or the death of one, is a moment when there is a touch of love and need deep enough to fan the faint hope. And so they stay. Others stay because the most they hope for is convenience, or comfort, or because anything is better than backyard gossip.

Psychologists tell us that the lowest rung on the ladder of emotional evaluation is the feeling, or rather the lack of feeling, which is called apathy. I agree that this is the saddest commentary one can hear regarding a marriage, that the people are apathetic toward one another. They continue to share a dwelling, but in reality they have neither a marriage nor a home.

It is sad because a very high percentage of these marriages started to be the fulfilment of heartfelt dreams, the biggest and best thing in life, and they have come to fit into the same category as the faded old bathrobe which continues to hang on the hook in the back of the closet. It is not used and enjoyed anymore, but it is not discarded to the rummage sale because of some nostalgic value which still clings to it. There seems to be a widespread notion that a marriage has a kind of fatalistic quality, that it is either going to be a good one or a bad one, depending upon whether the right two people get together in the first place, and that, if they do and each stays morally faithful, everything is bound to be all right.

Suppose you planted beside your front door a beautiful rose bush, and it was covered with lovely, fragrant blossoms. You noticed it as you passed it from time to time and were glad that it was there, everything about it was right. Suppose now, that time has passed—a good deal of it. One day you stop to take a closer look at the rose bush and discover to your dismay that the bush is dead. In careful retrospect, you realize that not once did you stop to cultivate, to prune, to fertilize, to water or nourish, or to care for the bush. You had simply been glad that it was yours, had thought it was nice having it there. But you had not made a conscious, thoughtful effort to keep it healthy. There was nothing wrong with the bush. It began as a healthy plant, full of promise for a productive, expanding existence. What happened was that it simply died of neglect. A few minutes' time each day spent in caring for the bush would have made the difference between the now dead plant, worthless and ready to be thrown away, and what it could have been, fulfilling the purpose for which it was intended.

It is exactly the same with a new marriage. What one has today depends almost entirely upon the amount of care which has gone into what one began with. Even a fine relationship, with everything going for it, will wither and die if it is neglected long enough, and conversely, a mediocre one will become deepened and enriched with sufficient "tender, loving care." A very high percentage of those washed-out, dreary marital messes are the result of just this kind of self-centered neglect.

It might be a good idea if you would stop today and take a closer look at the rose bush at your house and see if it might be drooping a little, looking a bit wan. You might, if you look closely enough, discover that it's heart is being attacked and seriously injured by a blight which is not easily visible from the outside appearance or at a casual glance. There may be a wee insect or a fungus which will eventually cause certain destruction, but which can be cleaned out and eradicated if the right antidote is used. That is, if the gardener is willing to roll up his sleeves, get to work and stay with it, and does not just stand there, looking sorrowful or swearing at the bugs. It takes a positive approach—diagnosis of the problem, determination of the best remedy, and, most importantly, action.

It is to help in taking these steps that this book is written. It is intended to be a practical look at a much-labored subject. Admittedly, it is not an all-purpose, handy guide to marital bliss but is, hopefully, a balanced, readable approach to the business of day-to-day life with a husband or a wife.

The things included here are not new, but they are real. Real, as opposed to theoretical, and they are the important things. I make this positive statement, not because of profound personal wisdom, but because the contents of this book are compiled from the broken pieces of life which have been brought, often in pain and tears, to my office for mending. I know these particular things are important because they are the things heard over and over, the things which happen to everyone.

The words used are not clinical, professional terms. They are, instead, daily bread-and-butter ones, the kind that life is lived by. Simple ones we use when we speak straight and direct and are more concerned with being understood than with sounding intellectual. There has arisen such a fog of high-sounding, complicated language and machinery around a troubled man and wife that it is a wonder they ever really find each other at all. This may, in some cases, be necessary, but it is more confusing than helpful. My intention is to wipe away a bit of this fog which has obscured the window through which marriage is viewed. When this is done, it is my hope that those who are interested enough to look will find that it is not a mirror which returns their own image, but a sparkling, clear glass which permits them to look beyond themselves into a wonderfully exciting existence.

It is my hope, also, that they will catch a glimpse of an occasional smile to enhance the picture.

2 Thank You, Dear

I have heard about a minister who takes quite seriously the responsibility which is his when he interviews a young couple before he performs their marriage ceremony. His time with them is not a few brief moments spent in arranging the complicated mechanics of how the job is to be done, but is instead, made rich and worthwhile by his wise counsel. Among a good many other potent little tidbits, he always includes this repartee (We will use John and Mary. John and Mary always seem to do everything.) "John, I want you to promise me that you will at all times be as courteous to Mary as you are to other men's wives." John nods and says, "Yes, sir." The minister then turns to Mary and asks her for the same promise. "Mary, I want you to promise me that you will at all times be as courteous to John as you are to other women's husbands." Mary, still single, breathless and wide-eyed, unhesitatingly answers yes.

Now, of course, all Johns and Marys are hardly more

19

than home from the honeymoon before they realize what an
impossible thing they have promised, but the idea deserves
some thinking about. The word "courtesy" is a kind of pink
and white, old-fashioned word, I guess, but the need for it is
just as acute and real as it ever was, always will be, long as
there are people. Ever spend an evening with a couple and
afterward find yourself wondering what on earth keeps
them together? Their whole purpose seems to be to see
which can needle the other the best. It's pick, pick, pick,
pick all evening long. Short jabs and long punches. The
only decision you can reach is that each knows it would give
the other too much pleasure if he were to leave. So the evil
game goes on. On the other hand, almost everyone knows
at least one couple who cause you to wonder in a different
way—a long-time couple, maybe even a golden-anniver-
sary one, who still have about them an air of sweetness, of
tenderness even. Spend five minutes with them and you
know that being in each other's company is a source of real
enjoyment for them. What accounts for the difference? Did
some star in heaven guide these two to each other and steer
them safely and serenely through many years of marriage
with no cause for irritation or selfishness? Not at all. I don't
mean there isn't a lot to be said for getting started with a
good partner as opposed to a poor one, but that is all it is,
just a start.

Most people agree that there is an atmosphere, an aura, a
sort of feeling that pervades a home or office, and the same
thing is true of a marriage. The relationship which exists
between a man and a woman who live together makes itself
felt. This aura follows the two outside the home and sometimes it is as recognizable as if a large label were printed on

their backs. A funny thing is that without really trying, you can think of a dozen cryptic labels for acquaintances. But it is surprisingly difficult to think of one which you feel is satisfactorily descriptive of your own marriage. Possibly because it is hard to be honest and flattering all in the same word. A little time spent in diagnosis of the atmosphere nearest *you* might be time well spent.

Suppose you do this, and discover that there has been a serious shortage of consideration one for the other and that the result is anything but an atmosphere of sweetness and light. What to do? Diagnosis is the first step, and the next one is to find an antidote. The radiant atmosphere of the beginning days of marriage is delicate and elusive unless it is guarded and preserved, and the preservative—the sweetner—is courtesy. There's not a trace left? Where do you suppose it went?

If someone you know makes a comment to you which you believe to be unkind or unfair, maybe even downright mean, and soon after an occasion presents itself for you to make a similar unkind comment, are you likely to do so? Human nature being what it is, you probably will. The pace is set, and like a merry-go-round, all it needs is an occasional shove by someone to keep it moving along in the same direction. Happily, the converse is also true. If the same person should make an unexpected complimentary remark to you, at the first opportunity you would please both yourself and your friend by returning the compliment.

It might be, that after a little retrospect, it will be pretty clear that the merry-go-round at your house is running along all right, but a bit in the wrong direction! If so, then somebody is going to have to put his foot out and bring it to a halt. Of course you don't get anyplace by standing still, so the next thing that needs to happen is that someone (probably the very same one who brought things to a stop) should give a good firm push in the opposite direction. The first push is the most important, of course, but no one can come up with one big enough or permanent enough to keep the apparatus going indefinitely. It takes many little boosts along the way—well-timed ones that come when they are needed.

We all know but seldom think about a basic theory, learned in Elementary Psychology: that one's treatment of another determines to a very great degree the kind of treatment he can expect to receive from that person. Funny thing, when you get right down to it, marriages, like all relationships, are made up of people. The chief difference is that the people involved in this one are those who have come together, almost always by choice, and have sworn publicly that it is their intention to hold this particular person in a very choice position for the remainder of life. This is further affirmed by a promise to love, to cherish, and to honor. Surely these high-sounding words mean a good deal more than simple good etiquette—the kind ordinarily shown a passing guest or a casual acquaintance. This one that has been singled out, chosen for one's own, can expect to be treated with more than ordinary courtesy. Yet, how many husbands and wives receive even half as much?

A businessman whose wife had complained of his terrible disposition justified it saying, "All day I am facing the public, smiling, no matter how I feel. When I get home, I am ready to quit playacting, and just be myself." Just by the way he said it, you could tell that to be himself was anything but pleasant. He is typical of many to whom good manners are like a garment which they put on as they leave the door of their home and always remove it just as they enter on their return. Some polite businessmen feel that part of the privilege of being the head of a household is the privilege of rudeness and lack of consideration to those who share the premises.

I know, and I'll bet you do too, a gay and charming young housewife who sparks up every gathering where she happens to be. I know something else about her, too. She takes her sparkle off with her hat when she get home. That great talent of hers of drawing people out of themselves, of giving of herself enthusiastically and gaily, this is all reserved for her "outside" self. This is for people she would like to impress, for those she wants to be sure will like and enjoy her. Why bother at home; here she can give way to all the selfish little vanities, be dull or mean, or anything else she happens to feel like being. After all, this is home; no need for pretense here.

Surely something is out of balance here; this logic just isn't logical. The law has historically protected with great care the privacy of the home and has safeguarded it from invasion of any kind. What goes on inside the walls of a domicile is to be controlled by those who dwell there. One of the cornerstones of privilege included in the maxim, "A man's home is his castle," is the right to determine the kind of conduct which is to be required therein—as long as there is no violation of the laws designed to protect the general health and safety, as these surround an individual no matter where he may be.

Home is the place of clean reality, where the game of

living takes place, and where the ground rules are to be made by the participants. Sometimes it seems that there are no rules at all and the whole business of being a family is a sloppy hodgepodge of uncontrolled persons trespassing upon one another. There isn't any activity, including just living, which runs as well without supervision and control as it does with a few well-defined, basic rules. If the goings on include more than one individual, then one of the first basics which needs to be understood by those involved is the quality of treatment each person can expect to receive from the other. This is important in all kinds of relationships, but more so in marriage than in any other. It has to be, because there is no other relationship which involves the same amount of sharing as is involved when two individuals decide to become one.

While it is more important to have a good understanding of individual privileges in marriage than most anywhere, there is almost sure to be a fairly well defined division of what is to be expected of each participant, of what each can reasonably expect of the other. Often, these matters are worked out in great detail to eliminate all possibility of either toe-treading or sidestepping. It is true that being in business with someone and still retaining his friendship requires some tricky footwork, but this isn't anything at all compared to the skill it takes to roll with the punches while discovering what it is like to be married. Almost everyone has had a wise grandmother who has warned: "You never really know a man till you are married to him." Almost no woman who has been a wife more than six days would disagree. The chivalrous gentleman of the courtship days often disappears pronto after the wedding, never to be seen again except in the presence of company in the home or when on display in public. In his place, for daily family fare, there is quite a different fellow.

Granny, if as fair as she was wise, would have to admit that a husband or two has been in for something of a jolt also. That fascinating, wide-eyed dancing partner and general all-round adoring one may have forgotten to say that she just simply cannot pull herself out of bed early enough to assemble a breakfast before her hero has to leave for work. She may possibly have overlooked a few other trifling bits of biographical information, such as a complete and total lack of comprehension of the purpose and/or care of such incidentals as money, kitchen ranges, automobiles, recipe books, charge accounts, brooms, and dustpans—not to mention a few leftover, past-due bills which accompanied her as an unsuspected dowry.

In addition, and in a way, the most surprising thing of all is that she seems to be equipped with a built-in switch. At a party she can, at will, become that gay, adoring pièce de résistance, and then can switch herself off just as the car pulls up in front of the house, and the evening is over. She doesn't seem to get turned on again until a guest appears or she has another night out. In between these times she is sullen, or impudent, as the mood strikes her. This she justifies by saying that at home she has the right to "be herself." The smiling, affable salesman, the warm, friendly, outgoing one whom everyone enjoys so much; used the same excuse for being rude and hateful to his family in private. He has a right to "be himself" at home; he isn't trying to sell anything, he says.

The shocked neighborhood cannot imagine what has

gone wrong with his wife when she files suit for divorce
from that "nice man." Little do they know that he gave his
customers and friends all his niceness and let loose all his
frustrations, hatreds, disappointments, and anger on his
family. This was what he called "being himself." Surely not.
This is really being the worst of himself. No reasonable man
and woman would, when planning their marriage, deliberately determine that their home life together would consist
of the worst personality traits possessed by each of them
running rampant and unrestrained. This is plain, naked
selfishness and will bear the dwarfed and bitter fruit which
is nourished by that climate.

Selfish disregard for the feelings of others is not what is
meant by "being able to enjoy the privacy of one's own
home." It does not imply a free license to live as selfishly or
violently as one might choose, with no obligations to re-
strain temper, or rudeness, or other bad character traits. It
is often just this lack of restraint that results in situations
which do call for a legal remedy. Terms such as "gross
neglect of duty," "extreme cruelty," "incompatibility," and
the like are used to describe actions which are the direct
outgrowth of selfishness, uncontrolled anger, and lack of
consideration for another.

The marriage contract, like any other, contains certain
terms, some clearly stated, some implied. Almost without
exception, each party to the contract makes a clear and
open statement, in fact a promise, to treat the other party
with honor. The universal method of showing honor to a
fellow being is to follow the simple rule which is often
called Golden—the kind of honest and fair treatment that
one enjoys receiving.

3 Hello There!

There is one belief which is shared in almost complete unanimity—except for the very young—and that is: Time passes ever more swiftly. I have often heard the statement made that the older we grow the more quickly it flies, and in many ways this is a disturbing thing to think about. For one who is already running behind, there would be comfort taken in the thought that some day there would be a designated catching up time but this apparently is not the case. The years do, indeed, go zipping by, and more rapidly than seems possible.

Soon little children are not hanging on Mother's hemline anymore; in fact they are not even around anymore. She no longer is running the taxi, the restaurant, the hotel, and general fix-it shop. She has known all along the time would come but surely not so soon. Suddenly, one day she looks across the breakfast table at her husband and realizes with a jolt that she and this man are alone. Totally, completely, utterly alone together! This thought may not be filled with the peace and contentment one would hope for; it might, rather, be more than a little disconcerting. This moment of truth may hold neither joy nor sorrow but may present disturbing, uneasy emotions and some questions without ready answers. Very likely, before she has pursued the subject more than a few minutes, she will have to face the fact that one thing that disturbs her is that this man is something of a stranger to her.

Doris, an attractive violin teacher in her forties, explained it this way, "Ted and I have about decided that we would be happier if we were to go our separate ways. Our children are both grown and married, and live out of state. We have no common interests anymore and do not seem able to enjoy each other's company. We are considering a divorce so that we will be able to try and find some sort of life for ourselves in another way." She admitted, upon questioning, that they had loved each other in the beginning and for the most part had had a good life together. Somehow during the years something had happened to their relationship, she said, and they had drifted so far apart that there seemed no meeting ground left. A later talk with Ted revealed that his feelings were very similar to those of Doris.

In answer to a direct question about what their idea of a good future would be, they each agreed that the best possible answer would be to somehow renew the old relationship they once had. Neither of them had become emotionally involved with anyone else, and they wanted to part only because the future together looked so bleak and lonesome. These two had been married more than twenty years and it was a long way back to the beginning, but through counseling we picked our way along carefully, uncovering the many little hurt places and the protective tricks which had hidden them. It had been a good marriage in the beginning, and it was so much worth the saving. Three years later a chance meeting with Doris found her still gratefully happy for the experience. She said that she and Ted had come to understand each other more completely than ever before.

The magic key which unlocked the door so long closed between these two was communication. For the first time in a good many years this husband and wife were able to talk to one another and actually be heard by the other. This is not as easy as it sounds.

If you are having trouble at your house getting an audience with your important person, it might be a good idea to answer a question for yourself: How easy are you to listen to? The first answer you will present to yourself is that you wouldn't yell if it weren't necessary in order to get someone to pay attention. Don't accept that one, be honest with yourself. A harsh, critical tone turns other people's ears off as quickly and as completely as pulling the plug disconnects the light.

If you managed to get by the first question, try this one: Have you a favorite subject matter? If so, it is quite likely that your erring mate can repeat with a good deal of accuracy what your little piece will be. Now there is another answer for this, and you know what it is. It wouldn't be necessary to repeat endlessly if you could have received some kind of response way back there. Right? Husbands don't generally use a nice phrase like "repeat endlessly." They use a nasty word like "nag." When I have an opportunity, I usually suggest to men that much of what they call nagging could be eliminated. Try listening to what she says.

It is harder to listen than to talk. It does seem, though, that some people make it even harder than it needs to be.

A defiant woman said to me once, "I'd just like to see you talk to my husband. I'd just like to see it. There's no way it can be done." She went on to say that when he was at home, he either had his nose in the newspaper, he was glued to the television, or he was asleep. "I might just as well not even be there." She said that occasionally when she just had to, she would grab him by the shoulders, look him straight in the face and say, "Now you are going to listen to me." She sighed and then said, "When I get all through, do you know what he says? All I get out of him is a little grunt. That's all, just a grunt."

Well, I listened to that woman. For almost forty-five minutes straight I listened, and I had a great feeling of sympathy for that husband. He knew very well what he was doing; the newspaper, the television, the quick nap—what wonderful escape mechanisms they were. She had the most unpleasant combination of shrill nasal tones, hypercritical attitude, and nonstop pace I have ever encountered. The thought of being subjected to that the first thing each morning and the last thing each night would chill even the implacable, scientific social worker. One might even look upon deafness with a certain amount of interest! This husband had done the next best thing; he had perfected what is known as "occupational" deafness.

Mothers with too many small children become expert at this, and it has saved the sanity of a good many. They learn to hear only the unusual sounds; the regular, everyday sounds slide right on by. Hearing is turned on and off at the discretion of the hearer—or nonhearer, as the case may be.

It is a great convenience; but, of course, a good deal of sound sneaks by unnoticed.

Some people even get so good at this that they catch just the tag end of voice tones and make a quick judgment as to whether some kind of answer is indicated and, if so, what it should be. It might be a slight chuckle, a little surprised noise, an agreeable uh-huh. I understand there are some who can do this for days and never get caught—that is, not till later when they don't know things they ought to know. Like a lot of other conveniences, the easy way doesn't always fit all occasions; and sometimes, there just isn't any substitute for hard work.

How difficult are you to listen to? One way to arrive at a fairly unbiased answer to that question is to ask yourself another: Do I have to repeat questions a lot? If you have trouble getting the important one at your house to talk with you, it might be a good idea to try listening to yourself for a while and see if you might make it a little less painful—especially if the subject before the house is an unpleasant one.

While you are in a self-examining frame of mind, with the hoodwinkers off, and willing to be brutally honest with yourself, go a step further. How are you at listening? Remember now, this is even harder to do well than talking. It requires the discipline of keeping your mouth shut on the quick little barbs that present themselves immediately in self-defense when your ego appears to be in jeopardy. It means looking interested even if your not; it means being receptive to another's ideas, complaints, or suggestions. In short, it means bringing yourself into subjection and permitting another to have complete self-expression while in the center of your full attention. A great majority of the people who have communication problems in their homes have them because they have not practiced the art of communicating.

"Every time we start to discuss a problem it ends up in a great big argument." This complaint is as widespread as the common cold, and sometimes it seems almost as contagious. I doubt that there is any more universal, more effective block to communication than the argument. Yet, interestingly enough, this can be a very useful means of getting information from one point to another. It is, like the surgeon's sharp-edged scalpel, a valuable tool when used with wisdom and skill, or an instrument of pain and destruction if used with heedless carelessness or with malice.

Since arguing is so well known to us all and so readily available, it would be well to be able to make the best use of the art. Everyone uses it anyway, so it might as well count for something. It will, if (1) the argument has a place of beginning and a place of ending; (2) if each person has heard what the other has said; (3) if in between the beginning and the ending something has been decided. If each of these things happens, then the time has been well spent. The sharp-edged tool has been effectively used and the general state of health is improved. An argument is almost certain to result if a statement is made which attacks the ego of the other, as the injured party will surely defend himself. What more instinctive way is there than to strike back at the attacker? Each learns the other's most vulnerable points, and the same battle is fought over and over. The argument then becomes a whip which is reached for upon the slightest provocation, not as a means of communication, but as a weapon with which to inflict pain.

The main reason most arguments accomplish nothing constructive is that everybody talks and nobody listens. This is especially true if the argument is a repeat. Each knows so well, probably almost word for word, what the other is going to say, and it is just a matter of waiting till one fellow is finished so the other can have his turn again. The waiting is done less and less patiently and, eventually, both are talking at the same time, each trying to speak loud enough to be heard over the other. And all the time nobody is listening, except the neighbors. Naturally it is impossible that this kind of communication could solve any differences, because neither person has heard anything the other has said. Both just take offense all over again because of the stirring up of the unpleasant emotions. The shouting does not cease because the problem has been solved, but because of a fortunate interruption or because one or both have run out of insulting things to say. Sometimes the feeling of hopelessness is so complete that the struggle to continue quarreling is just not worth the effort it takes. And so another brick has been laid upon the wall between two people who at one time whispered lovingly to each other about every detail of life.

After this episode has been repeated enough times to establish a pattern, each knows what to expect from the other and is rarely surprised at the sequence of events. About the only variance is the degree of hostility which is expressed. Often at this time, one of the parties becomes sufficiently concerned to attempt a worthwhile, serious conversation with the idea of actually accomplishing some degree of understanding, only to find the other completely uncooperative.

After a few unsuccessful attempts, a friend or confidant is sure to hear, "I just can't talk to him anymore. He refuses to discuss our problem. It's like talking to a brick wall." This is a very accurate statement; this individual has surrounded himself with a protective shell, behind which he retreats whenever certain dangerous sounds are heard. Once this wall has been completed, with every stone carefully cemented into place, and no doors or openings remaining, it is a difficult thing indeed to find a loose stone somewhere which will permit entry. There almost always is one, but sometimes the patient search which is required to find it takes more time than there is.

It is still examination day; try this one. How many minutes a day do you and your marriage partner talk to each other? That's an easy one, you think, but I mean really talk. Let's make it a little harder. Eliminate all discussions having to do with the government, the relatives, the children, the business, religion, and the weather. Now, try again. How much do you talk to each other daily? Probably not at all if you are like most people. No one but you two knows why you got married, but it is a safe bet that one of the things that figured in it was that you like so much to be together. You were good company, nice to be with, good to talk to.

The reason this is so important is that this is the way you keep in touch, the way you keep acquainted. Just sharing a house doesn't do it. You need to keep track of each other as individual people, not just as mother or father or even husband and wife, but as person.

This business of communication unfortunately does not take care of itself automatically. In fact, it seems to demand a good deal of tending to. The best way of tending it is like tending to paying the bills, brushing your teeth, or growing a garden—that is by having a certain time for it. It sounds silly, I suppose, to plan a time to talk to the person you live with, and yet I mean just that. Start today. If your mate is the sort of person you can discuss it with, do so; otherwise, decide for yourself.

Consider your schedule and choose fifteen minutes out of your day which will belong to the two of you. Perhaps just before you part for the morning, or just after dinner is finished. Shoo the children out to play, pour another cup of coffee and visit. Maybe just after you have gone to bed— the lights are off and there will be no interruptions. It doesn't matter when, so long as somewhere there are some minutes with a circle around them that belong to no one else. They will come to be the most valuable time of the day if you use them right. This is the time that a husband can know he has his wife's complete, undivided attention. For some men this is a hard thing to come by, especially those who have small children.

There is an expression "listening with half an ear"; well, you can't really listen with only half an ear, or even with a whole ear, or even with two whole ears. To really listen it takes both ears and the whole mind. When you listen with your ears, your mind, with your entire full attention, then you hear not only the words, but also what they mean, what they say. You hear sometimes the things which are not actually said, but only wished; you hear many things which would be missed if you were listening only with ears. Most important of all, the one who is speaking is aware that he, at that moment, possesses your entire attention, and he will want to make it count for the very most. Here you can reach each other. Make these moments your time to share the day, whatever it contains—not necessarily the trouble time of the day. On the other hand, many problems have minute beginnings and can easily be taken care of if they are not allowed to grow and eventually mature into full-sized misunderstandings which bear offsprings of all kinds.

Determine within yourself that every day you and your mate are together, there will be at least ten or fifteen minutes that will belong exclusively to the purpose of keeping you in open communication. Could be, some days you will not speak much during those minutes, but you both will know that the time is there, set apart, and available. This one step can determine whether that wall goes higher and higher, or whether it develops a great big crack which weakens it so that eventually it crumbles and falls, giving free access to the one behind it. If your timing is good, these precious moments may keep a wall from being built at all.

4 When Father Comes Marching Home

Sometimes it comes out early and easily, just a flat solid statement, and sometimes it comes awkwardly and painfully after a long time. But, sooner or later, one complaint is almost always uttered by the husbands who have sat across the desk from me. Occasionally one of them may be belligerent and defiant about it, but not usually. More often they think it is not manly to care about it, so they pretend they don't really mind, until the time for pretending is past. And when he is sitting there in the green chair, that time is past and there can be nothing but truth. So, the truth comes, all at once or in little bits and pieces; but adding up to the same answer.

Charles said it well, simply and clearly: "You know, when I get home after work the only one who acts as if she cares at all is my little dog. She really is glad to see me, and lets me know it. Maybe everybody is. I don't know, but you can't tell it. I always come in the back door because Doris is in the kitchen about then, usually. But she always looks up from whatever she is doing with the most startled look, and says, 'Oh, are you home?' She says it like she really means, 'Surely you're not home already!' Somehow she makes me feel like I've done the wrong thing just by getting home. I used to try and say hello to the kids, but I don't do that anymore. Seems I would get between them and the TV set at just the wrong minute, and the darned thing was on so loud they couldn't hear what I said anyway—when they were home, that is, which they usually weren't. So now, I just pick up little Suzy, my dog, stick her under my arm and go out in the yard. I act like I don't care—and maybe I shouldn't really—but I do. It gives me the feeling that all I am hanging around there for is just to pay the bills and keep the place up. You know, I believe that if the bills were taken care of and nothing broke, I'll bet you I could be gone for a whole week and nobody would even notice it."

Charles felt like stomping his feet and yelling, "Hey, please somebody, look happy just a little that I have come home again. Don't shut me out. Doggone it, I'm glad to be here; somebody be glad with me." But he was an uncomplicated, well-mannered man, and instead of stomping and yelling, he quietly swallowed his hurt, put the little dog under his arm, and went out into the backyard to play with her. The hurt pride didn't disappear though but followed the course of many small hurts which, through repetition, grow into resentment.

The sequence of events which followed, and which finally led Charles and Doris to seek counseling, was as natural as could be. Charles began to stop occasionally for a beer on the way home from work. No one noticed at first, but his arrival began to be less and less dependable and Doris fussed over delayed meals. The scene was repeated so many times that, often, by midafternoon they each began to get tense and agitated just thinking ahead to how unfair the other was going to be in a few hours.

Ironically, Doris had become convinced by this time that Charles really no longer cared for her, or he would respect her wishes instead of deliberately doing something which she had repeatedly asked him not to do. The very same emotion—hurt pride—which had started the whole unhappy merry-go-round, added the impetus. When it was all unraveled, it looked kind of silly. They both thought so and laughed a little, but it was a painful time for them and really quite unnecessary.

Charles and Doris were not a couple of screwballs; they were apple-pie normal. True, a good communications system would have solved the problem at it's beginning when it was just a misunderstanding, but everyone is so afraid of appearing childish.

Perspective is a word with a thousand applications and yet is difficult to apply effectively when related to oneself. Since we are neither Charles nor Doris, perhaps we can. Doris, for example, lost perspective and forgot just why it was that she was so busy just at the time Charles got home every day. The clutter, the children, the phone, and the dinner—all seemed to need attention at just the moment he came in the door. The too-hot dryer was ruining the drip dry things and the still frozen meat seemed to be looking at her with an implacable expression.

Sometimes, she thought, he just waited outside the house till the most awful moment of the day and then walked in looking for all the world as if he thought someone was going to hand him a prize for something. She felt overcome with frustration, and it showed on her face. Charles saw it, misread it, and thought it was intended for him. If Doris' perspective had been standing there, nice and straight, instead of crosswise, she would have taken three or four minutes—maybe even less—just enough to dry her hands, flash Charles her nicest welcome, smile and give him a small, "Hi, I'm glad you're home." There would still be two minutes left for a good fast hug.

Admittedly, Charles's perspective could have done with a bit of adjusting also. He would have acted differently if his attention had not been focused so completely upon himself. Rather than being aware of only his disappointment, he would have seen the cause of Doris' dismay. Rather than swallowing hurt pride and walking on through the room, he would have stopped beside her for a moment, long enough to leave a short kiss. "Come on along and talk to me while I change. Another minute or two won't make that much difference. I'm glad to be home, doll." This was Charles' thought, but Doris didn't have time for mind reading.

Most grown-up married boys and girls have carefully tucked away in a secret treasure chest a beautiful romantic notion of how it is supposed to be when they and their chosen lover meet after an endless day of separation. There is usually a dreamy, ethereal quality to the meeting, helped along by a hint of soft background music, a decanter of wine, and a low couch. According to this childish, fanciful notion, the husband and wife, who continue to resemble a shiny new bride and groom, greet each other ecstatically, and wander arm in arm toward the couch where they pledge their love anew.

This isn't the kind of thing you can get people, even happy ones, to admit right out loud. But, admitted or not, the dream is there—a lot or a little. Maybe all that is left is a kind of used-to-be wish. Nothing wrong with this, really, if the dream grows up or if it actually comes true every year or so at anniversary time. Or if you can remember it and laugh, it won't carry any hurt at all. But, if you try to make it fit real life, it just won't; and the ever widening gap between the two can stretch into a hurting place.

Any wife, after a day spent playing "now they're clean now they're dirty" with several dozen diapers, chasing, feeding, spanking, and soothing a few assorted children; making PTA cookies, finding the lost jacket, dodging the telephone and the doorbell, and who still manages to be above panic or despair, is a solid gal indeed. The idea of making herself desirable, or even presentable, couldn't possibly merit consideration, even if it were to occur. She had promised herself to stop at four, make a fast roundup of living room clutter, and here it was five minutes till five. There's no doubt this would be the night he would be extra hungry, and she was not only out of ideas but groceries as well. Scrambled eggs once more!

It hadn't been two days ago she had promised this would never happen to her again. Funny thing, here she had been functioning at top efficiency all day. Now all at once, when she realized how both she and the situation were sure to appear to her husband, she began to have that strange "failure feeling" that started somewhere in her stomach. She felt small and weak, ineffective, as if part of her wasn't turned all the way on. There was sure to be trouble or that awful quietness.

Probably no man expects to arrive home from his day's work to find his children all standing in a row, scrubbed and shining, waiting for a pat on the head. Neither does he expect to open the door and find his wife there, exotic and glamorous, waiting to shower him with kisses and attention. I do believe, however, that the arrival home is something looked forward to by most men, and it should be one of the nicest moments of the day. Think it smacks a little of the conquering hero returning from the fields of battle? Very likely it does, and the similarity may not be entirely accidental. The weapon may be a draftman's pencil or an order book, a surgeon's knife or welding torch. It may be as far removed from the warrior's sword as a book of philosophy or a carpenter's saw, but it serves the same purpose. It is the implement he uses to do battle.

The amount of success he has in his use of it determines how well he can provide for his family. There is not as much drama as in the old days of knighthood, but certainly the need to be a winner is still there—particularly in some highly competitive fields where the attitude of rivals is almost cannibalistic. The breadwinner who does not fit into this picture at all is the one who is in a job situation with too much security. There he fights another enemy more seductive and deadly than any other—boredom. But no matter who the foe, whether vanquished or victorious, the one who went out to do battle should be privileged to return to his private domain and be accepted with honor and dignity. No big show, but some sign of gladness.

5 Just a Bag of Jelly Beans

Girls are, it seems to me, a good deal like puppy dogs in some ways. (Girls, meaning all females—even wives.) Occasionally, they just have to be patted on the head, or elsewhere, and told how cute they are. Maybe not regularly, or even often, but once in a while. It really takes very little to inspire a tremendous response in a little brown-eyed Bassett. Pick him up, let him know in his favorite way that you really are aware of him—a little manhandling, a scratch behind the ear, some sweet talk—then watch the magic result. He will turn handsprings with glee, wiggling excitedly.

It may be carrying the parallel a bit far to expect to see your wife leaping or wiggling about the room; but, unless you are still waging an already lost battle, there will be some kind of response. It takes such a little bit to make her happy, but that little bit is mighty important. There is a lot of loose talk about how important a mink coat is to a woman, and I certainly don't intend to quarrel with that idea, but there are many times when just a bag of jelly beans could accomplish a miracle.

An amazing number of women tell me that their husbands never remember birthdays or anniversaries. Some are openly bitter about it, others matter of fact, some pretend not to mind at all. But, when the truth is finally told, it does matter and matter much. Ironically, there are some husbands who never miss a birthday or an anniversary, but it doesn't really advance their cause a bit. On the morning of the big day the wife recognizes that look and it doesn't take a mind reader to know what he is thinking: "I must remember to stop on the way home tonight and pick up a box of candy for Marge. Today's her birthday." She not only knows what he is thinking, she knows what kind of candy it will be—soft centers, the kind he likes best, and he will finish the top layer before he goes to bed.

Chances are she will say nothing and will smile and try to look pleased when he hands the box to her. Then, a couple of days later, the bewildered husband confides to his buddy that he doesn't know what has gotten into Marge, she's cross as a bear. Marge, or almost any other wife, does not expect a glamorous, expensive gift, especially when she knows the budget won't accomodate it. What she does want is recognition of her importance to an important person. I suppose this is probably a childish hangover from little girls days, but it does matter. Indeed it does! The way a girl figures is that special days are set apart so that someone can show her in a special way that she is special. If it doesn't happen, she is likely to conclude either that she really isn't special or that she is and he just doesn't know it. Either way, it is not a happy conclusion. It sits crosswise and makes for uneasiness.

It has been trite for the last hundred years or so to say that the thought matters more than the gift, but it still is just as true as it ever was. A pair of fuzzy slippers or a single red rose can mean more than a gift costing many times as much, if the one who receives it knows it was purchased for the special joy that it would bring. The idea of someone not caring enough to bother, or of picking up something just because he feels he has to is what hurts. Sure it costs a little; but, if the price tag reflects more in time and thought than in dollars, that "basset-hound wiggle" you will get will be even wigglier. Oh, I've *heard* of females who were insulted with a gift not up to a certain price standard and, also, of some who were bored with lavish gifts and Paris originals because they weren't picked out personally by hubby, but I've never *met* any of them.

There are some good, solid old husbands who look on this sort of thing as a lot of woman nonsense and are fond of saying, "Gladys knows I love her. I wouldn't have stuck around the last twenty years if I didn't." There usually is a jaunty chuckle accompanying this bit of philosophical wisdom, and Gladys is supposed to feel warm and gratified and maybe even say something nice. The funny part is that there are lots of Gladyses who actually do, who are wise enough to know the truth of the statement and to know that this is as close as they will ever come to hearing an expression of love.

There are, of course, countless ways of showing love, and I am for every one of them, including the plain old, "I love you." Sure, people can add things up and come up with the right answer, but, as in most other things, the simple, direct way is usually best. And it might help her to know that she is getting the right answers in the adding up she does. Some husbands have even learned that it doesn't have to be an "either-or" situation. Besides occasionally saying those lovely little pink and white words, there are lots and lots of other ways of saying exactly the same thing.

Fortunately, it doesn't require a genius to do this. In fact, it is the easiest part about being a husband; but it sometimes turns out that it is so easy it just doesn't get done. Somehow, the business of just ordinary, everyday living seems to keep people occupied and, without anybody thinking about it much, another half-dozen weeks have gone by. So there we are, back to special days again. You see, we need them. It is so nice to have a day all picked out for you to give you the chance you need to pause long enough to say an extra nice thank you for the ordinary things.

A wise someone once wrote a song, "Try a Little Tenderness." Women are absolute suckers for tenderness. A true-blue gal will stick with a fellow through almost anything as long as she is convinced that he really loves her and really needs her. And if, once in a while, he will look right straight at her, smile a little, and say, "You're tops," she'll start all over again. It's only when she begins to feel that he never really sees her, or really wouldn't miss her until he needed the dishes or laundry done, that she gets hard to live with.

Sometimes women feel compelled to dream up some pretty wild tricks to pull just so they will be noticed—like orange hair or polka-dot pants. There is a certain amount of routine or monotony connected with any job which is done on a daily basis, and housework is certainly no exception.

One would be hard put to find challenges, rewards, and incentives in devoting hours of close comradeship to dust-cloths, mops and brooms, baskets of dirty clothes to be washed, and baskets of wrinkled clothes to be ironed—particularly when there is no end product and no hope really of ever being finished with anything. Doing housework is very much like stringing beads with no knot in the end of the string!

Even the person who has a monotonous assembly-line job at least has a change of scene: he has a time of leaving and a time of arriving, a time of beginning and of quitting. The housewife is supposed to just keep on keeping on, weekends included. I do not mean to portray the American homemaker as a member of a downtrodden, deprived minority. On the contrary, the majority of them have a number of efficient tools and appliances which cut to a minimum the amount of hard physical labor required to keep a dwelling clean. She can also feed her family and do the laundry with far less effort than her grandmother did. In many ways, the American housewife is the most blessed of all women, and she is envied throughout a great part of the world. Most of them are aware of this and wouldn't trade jobs with anyone. This attitude would be shared by a lot more housewives if their husbands could understand how very simple it would be to add a few fringe benefits.

There is no job which, by its nature requires a more humble, self-giving attitude than do the menial tasks that wives and mothers do for other people. Following after people and cleaning their clothes and bathtubs, mending their rips and tears with needles and Band-Aids, sweeping their crumbs and pressing their pleats—these are things women do. They collect recipes, buy food, mix it and fix it, cook it and share in its goodness. Then all at once another meal is over and there is nothing left but a tableful of ugly, dirty dishes. Now, there may be a more depressing sight somewhere in the world, but not if you are a woman—especially if you contemplate the apparent idiocy of your role. It was your own time and energy which got this hodgepodge of things together, and now you must spend almost as long in making it go away—and all so that a few selected human beings will have a satisfied feeling in their innermost parts.

Very likely, sometime before she comes face to face with the sun again, this woman will sleep beside her husband and, even then, will continue to provide for his needs. And then morning, and another day. This one for the things she didn't get done the day before, along with many of the ones she did. Honor, prestige, accumulated leave, paid holidays, promotions? No, afraid not. Yet there is a big demand for the job. Always has been and, I suppose, there always will be. It's those fringe benefits. It isn't the base pay, for sometimes that is very poor indeed. It certainly isn't because the hours are good. You're never off duty.

The attraction is not the hope of fame or glory. The appeal that the job of homemaker has is an irresistible one —the opportunity to give oneself completely in loving service to another. And it can stay that way—loving service instead of drudgery and monotony—if the chief executive will see to it. When the work a person does is not exciting or even very interesting in and of itself, then the incentive has to come from outside the actual activity or performance of it. If the incentive is there, a woman will do anything and do it her very best. It doesn't take much. For shining windows, a good meal, a scrubbed linoleum, hard things well done, anything from a simple thank you to a whopping big, "Wow! You're terrific!" would be a very satisfactory pay check. Otherwise about this time a wife begins to think of herself as having melted into the design of the wall paper. Or she may consider fixing herself a slot in the broom closet and taking up abode with the other inanimate utensils.

"Here, let me help you." "Nobody makes an apple pie like you do." "How do you get so much done and still look so darn cute?" "Sue, you've polished this old room till it is lovely." For words like these, a wife will zoom like a little robot, hum a song, and have a kiss waiting. The only good thing about this kind of work is the knowledge that you have pleased someone. Any ordinary, run-of-the-mill, half-awake husband could, with a dozen or so well-chosen words, have a wife who would enjoy her job of homemaker. It is so simple and it requires so little of him—just a little thoughtfulness, just a little tenderness, just a bag of jelly beans.

6 Here a Penny, There a Penny

I believe it would require a considerable search to find a half-dozen adults of sound mind who would disagree with the statement that, at some time or other, nearly every married couple faces a problem directly connected with money. The problem is not always the lack of money; it may be over what to do with the unclaimed excess. I have even heard there are some who have such a quantity that this in itself is a considerable problem, but I don't *know* anyone who has had any serious worries as a result of such a delightful situation. Alas, it is far more likely that trouble comes from the other side of the ledger.

Typical, average, usual, ordinary, common—choose any one of these adjectives and it will fit as a description of money problems in marriage. And you can keep the same word and apply it neatly to describe the likelihood that the money problem in question will be caused by a shortage, either slight or substantial. "Where did it go?" "How could you have gone through so much so soon?" "How can you expect me to do what I have to do on this?" "Can't you find some way to cut down?" Questions like these fly round and round the room. And the one who is supposed to answer usually cannot because, for most folks, there just aren't any good answers to these questions. Not unless the money handler happens to be blessed with a good, sharp pencil, a columnar pad, a high IQ, and an income to match.

There is almost sure to be a wide gap in understanding if a husband-breadwinner comes home, gives the check to little Dolly Dimple, but doesn't have any knowledge of how it is divided. It is quite a jolt to him when he decides to cut loose a little and buy a new boat trailer, or a pinstriped suit to go to the convention, or to build a new porch on the house after all, and then discovers that the little nest egg, which he had supposed *they* were accumulating, apparently is snuggling in someone else's nest. Some men persuade themselves that their little sleight-of-hand brides must be slipping it out the back door to strangers, or even worse.

No one can really blame them, because it *is* hard to understand how quickly money disappears. The only way to convince a doubter is with facts. There probably are more unkept budgets than there are unkept anything else, but there is a real necessity for some kind of record of what, where, and why. The Internal Revenue Service is even more curious than husbands are, so there really is no one who will believe you.

Having the husband pay the bills may not be the easy answer because, if a wife neither earns the money nor has control of it at any time, it is expecting a lot to hope that she will be understanding about the "underage" when she thought for sure there was some "overage." This is the fertile soil in which a first suspicion gets planted. It has been known to grow to an absolute certainty that there is a love tryst with a kept woman somewhere, or that he has taken up gambling. "Heaven knows, *I* don't spend anything." Here again, a nice, well-kept set of cancelled checks or bills marked PAID is the unarguable answer—unless, of course, that little seed of suspicion had more than "supposing" to grow on, and the way she added things up happened to be just the way to come up with the right answer.

Who should pay bills and keep records is a question which must be answered by each couple for themselves, and often after a good deal of trial and error. The fact that they were brought up to think it should be done a certain way does not always mean that way will work for them. We all know well-qualified, successful businessmen who are capable of making very handsome salaries, but who are not reliable when it comes to paying their own bills. They miss past due notices, never take advantage of discount opportunities, pay some bills twice and others not at all. These are details which get overlooked in the hustle for bigger things. A man of this type, hopefully, would be blessed with a wife who is both able and willing to assume the job of treasurer and paymaster. If she has poor money sense, it is a solid gold certainty that, when the day of reckoning comes and that nice round salary check just didn't get the job done, they will each blame the other for the hole in the bucket— and the battle horn has sounded!

I don't know that anyone has done a study on the question, but it seems to me that many more women manage the family exchequer than men. Sometimes, the job comes to them by default, and they do it because if they don't no one will. Sometimes, a harried husband hopes it will teach his wife an appreciation for the family finances and help curtail her extravagances. Sometimes, after a frank appraisal, a man admits that his wife just naturally does a better job of it.

Whatever the basic reason, there is a fringe benefit in most instances. This responsibility helps to defeat the notion which occurs to every housewife now and then, that she is really just a glorified housekeeper. To be handed a certain amount of money on a certain day to do certain things adds to this feeling. She has a different feeling if she has a part in the handing out. For some women, who have to operate on a catch-as-catch-can basis, to have a certain sum would be a great delight.

Each couple must do their own deciding. Let's face it, there are fad-happy gals who could no more be trusted with the family checkbook than with the free run of Fort Knox. It is almost inevitable that there will be trouble in a household like that unless the wife is willing to admit that money handling is not one of her talents, or unless she is married to a man who can manage the money with a good firm rein without being miserly toward her—maybe even saving up so that she can have an occasional splurge.

It is not uncommon for a wife to go on a shopping spree, even when she knows they can't afford it, as a way of paying back her husband for a particular hurt he has dealt her. This is a little like the old quip about cutting off ones nose to spite his face, as she is sure to feel the resulting bind as much as her husband is.

Sometimes the checkbook becomes a "get-even weapon" in a real sense of the word. Who can point a finger of blame at a woman who finally provides herself with a nice treat of some kind after having watched her husband take his lovely new, expensive rifle and go off on a week-long hunting trip with "the boys?" He's pretty sure to be the kind that pats her on the hand and tells her to be good while he is gone. She very likely will, especially as he has left her without a car and with the four children. The first couple of times this happens, it goes pretty well and before long there is a little arrangement about it—never spoken but just there, accepted by the husband and resented by his wife.

Eventually she will fight, and her weapon may very well be money. Sometimes, the fight may be caused by the expensive, selfish, overconsumption of alcohol which the family cannot afford, or by a leftover adolescent passion for new automobiles. But, as long as there is not a mutual understanding and agreement about all matters related to the money belonging to the family, there will be unsettled business before the house.

While it may be hard to come to this plateau of agreement when the income is from just the husband, it is usually made more difficult when there are two incomes—that of the husband and of his working wife. This is not to say it is impossible, however. Every neighborhood has many examples of families who have flourished and enjoy high achievements which otherwise could not have been accomplished. A blanket indictment against women being both wives and job holders is unrealistic because there are successful examples on every hand. Often, the success of the venture is due to the mature, balanced judgment of the husband who realizes that with the shared privileges of an increased total income go the shared responsibilities for the care and feeding of his family. He willingly assumes his share, or at least a good part, of the things that have to be done in any household, and he does so with no fear of losing his masculinity. This kind of arrangement, with the money going into commonly agreed goals, can be most successful.

But, what about the home where the husband does believe that this sharing idea does not carry over into all areas, that the kitchen is off limits to anyone of the male gender, and that contact with washing machines, brooms, vacuum cleaners, and the like is to be avoided as completely as possible? Yet, his wife is employed outside the home. If he prefers that she not work elsewhere, this can be an effective way to discourage it. But, if he favors her being employed, enjoys the financial help which it provides, and still maintains this attitude, the responsibilities are rather badly out of balance.

This is, however, not an uncommon attitude and is believed by many to manifest some sort of manliness. Most anyone can think of a better name for it than that. The arrangement in this kind of household means that friend wife arrives home from work, changes her clothes, and heads for the kitchen to begin the second shift, while friend husband grabs the newspaper with a great sigh of gratitude that another day of work is finished. He does manage to muster up enough leftover physical stamina to make it to the table when he is informed that dinner is ready.

If the weather is right, he might even make a half-dozen trips around the yard on the lawn mower. His interest in keeping the yard looking nice has glimmered a bit more brightly since he can *sit* on a lawn mower (looking very pleased with himself) that he was shrewd enough to trade off for that old one he used to have to *walk* behind. The combination of the outdoor air and all this exertion are sure to make him snooze before the television set a little later. He may wake up occasionally and wish that Dot would get through with whatever it was she always seemed to be doing and come sit with him. When Dot finally gets this day taken care of, makes the necessary preparation for the next one, and climbs wearily into bed, this very same husband is the guy who gets his feelings hurt when she declines his proposition of lovemaking. He turns over and goes to sleep muttering to himself about the problems of being married to a cold potato.

Difficult as this woman's role may be, there is one which far exceeds it. Our world is filled today with occupations which call for the greatest contribution mankind has to offer. Challenges are made to men and women alike to pledge their energies, their hearts and minds to tasks which seem unattainable, in fields of science, education, medical research and practice, creative arts, and many others. But there is one challenge which surpasses them all. The most surprising thing of all is the number of women who accept the challenge, and some of them even actually achieve success. Unfortunately, for every success, there are many who miss the mark. This most difficult of all things to do is attempted every day by more and more women, the majority of them totally unqualified even to begin. I am talking about one woman trying to do successfully three full-time jobs within a twenty-four-hour period. I am talking about one woman being simultaneously a wife, an employee, and a mother.

Very rare, indeed, is the woman who can give her em-

ployer a productive eight-hour day, come home and be an
adequate mother to her children, and still manage to find
time to be the wife her husband desires. I am not saying it
cannot be done, because it is, but darned seldom. It requires
extraordinary cooperation on the part of the entire family,
great organization of household, and marvelous dispositions
on the part of both husband and wife. This last requirement
is hard enough to find in one person. To find it in two is
almost impossible. What happens, is that one usually comes
out on the little end; somebody gets cheated at least a little.

Chances are, it isn't going to be the boss because he
controls the pay check. He gets the best eight hours, and
next to him will come the children. They are usually quite
vocal about their needs and are in varying degrees of help-
lessness. Besides, most mothers have a real desire to do
these things. So here dear old friend husband is, last in line.
Mom hopes he is understanding and patient, and he is—
and helpful too. But, snitches and snatches of her time may
not always be enough. Fine, hairlike cracks may soon begin
to appear in that smooth relationship; and, with sufficient
joggling and insufficient patching, a real honest-to-goodness
crack may continue to deepen until it is openly discernible.
It may eventually become an actual break.

When a husband begins to feel neglected and displaced,
it generally makes him feel pretty uncomfortable and unhappy. He does not, however, tap his busy wife on the
shoulder and say, "Look, look sweetie. I'm still here. Remember me? I miss you." Nothing so simple as that. Instead, he either gets grouchy, or drunk, or finds other places
to be rather than home. Sometimes his out-of-place feeling
will take a bizarre direction if the situation continues long

enough that it becomes painful and if his psychological
makeup is such that he feels unable to openly challenge it.
Window-peeking, shoplifting, fascination with antisocial
pastimes of all sorts are sometimes traceable results of the
loss of self-esteem. More likely, however, is a general deteri-
oration of the tone of the marriage atmosphere. The joy of
the union is no longer there, as there is not sufficient union
to be joyful about.

Saddest of all is the fact that, often, this tremendous
strain is placed upon a marriage when there is no financial
necessity for it. Surely no outsider may presume to tell a
wife when she should or should not work, but there are
signposts of danger along the way that ought to be pointed
out. Too bad there isn't a little somebody, who would
appear at just the right moment, blow a whistle, wave a flag,
ring a bell, or somehow or other flash a warning finger at
the trouble spot, and a good smooth repair job could be
accomplished.

But there is a way.

In the absence of such helpful little pixies, some com-
mon-sense addition and subtraction will have to do. There
is just so much of Mother to share and just so much time in
which to do the sharing. Is there one brave enough to step
forward and declare that she has divided herself into three
portions to the full satisfaction of all? If so, then congratu-
lations, highest hurrahs, and *cum laude* galore, because
here is one with intelligence, extraordinary energy, held
charmingly on course with wit and romance. If she has
managed this, there is still one person who is not being
given any time in this merry-go-round schedule, and that is
she, herself. Every individual must add up to something

more than useless scraps that aren't big enough to put together.

Nothing we do is as important as the reason for our doing it. If this pace is necessary in order that children be fed or have good medical and dental care, or to get debts off the conscience and ledger, or because Father is ill and cannot pull his share, then the sacrifices should be made and shared by all. Then the sense of individual loss is eased, because each knows that this is part of his contribution to the family effort. He simply uses better and enjoys more the time there is to be shared.

This same oneness of purpose cannot exist, however, if Mom is working because she thinks she is going to seed around the house, or because this year's cars are cuter than last, or because the children make her nervous. Sometimes, she seeks employment because of a husband who does not have the get-up-and-get-out to provide the level of living she would enjoy. In that case, she probably will be less frustrated if she is working than if she were home worrying about it.

An ideal answer to this problem is the part-time job. While it is not available to all women, it has worked out very satisfactorily for many. There are few things I have ever felt tempted to crusade about, but the virtues of part-time work outside the home, or even at home for that matter, need a Clara Barton or a Florence Nightingale. The unused talents of womenfolk restlessly locked in homes is sufficient to dream, build, and efficiently operate entire cities. The only way to draw it out and make use of it is by educating employers to the value of the part-time worker. The average employer thinks only of a "half-day" worker, but ever more popular would be the two- or three-day-a-week job.

The self-employed woman is probably the most likely of all to find real fulfilment in her working situation, as her hours are more within her control than they might otherwise be. Many women run a business from their homes. Thus, they can be readily available to their families when needed. Others—and this I have found most satisfactory for myself—have certain days in every week which are office days and certain other days which are marked for "at-home" days.

Each family must make its own decision for itself, but for sure it must be just that—a family decision, entered into by all who will be affected. Most children, if asked, would prefer more Mom than more things which Mom's money will buy. But let *them* say—and Daddy's vote ought to count double.

7 In-Law, Outlaw

I guess that being a good in-law is just about the hardest thing there is to do. It must be, or there would be a few more good ones around. This isn't the kind of thing on which percentages are available, but one doesn't have to spend very many days in the domestic relations business to discover that the trouble is more likely to be "in-law" than almost anything else. And it is a little more likely to be mother-in-law than father-in-law. In fact, I have about decided that all the mother-in-law jokes I have ever heard are all true. Funny thing, too, because, taken individually, they are generally very nice people.

It is when they put on the "mother-in-law hat" that something dreadful happens. Very rarely is their motive bad. Usually, they want nothing but the best for their children, sometimes even for their children's spouses, but the damage they do while going about their good works is unbelievable. Many times, the trouble begins just before or just after the marriage, when the new member of the family is given the idea that he or she is not as welcome as might be. This impression can easily leak through the polite amenities. Nothing is clearly spoken which can be challenged, but the meaning is crystal clear: "I won't fight you, my dear, in fact I will do my best to tolerate you, but please understand that you are not the one I would have chosen." The new bride or groom gets the message, and the defenses immediately go up. The battle lines are drawn, and a new marriage is begun with one strike decidedly against it. Later, when the trouble becomes serious enough to erupt the polite surface, the other spouse, blissfully unaware that sides were chosen in the very beginning, will be astonished, dismayed, or angered—depending on his temperment—and is certain to chalk the whole idea up to jealous imaginings. And so, a little wedge has been placed between the two, a small feeling of resentment, of not being understood.

In-laws cannot cause trouble, no matter what they do, as long as a husband and wife stand together, each upholding and supporting the other's view. It is when one or the other takes a position alongside the in-law, and the line-up is three on one side against one lone fellow on the other, that a marital problem is the certain result. Many of these little battles run along for years, but they really become hard to hide when children come along. Then, suddenly, in addition to being in-laws, these same people are grandparents. While they may double the joys in a good situation, they will almost surely double the woes in a bad one.

It is considered the inherent right of grandparents to spoil their grandchildren, and most parents expect this to at least some degree. But some grandparents abuse their special privilege and use children as pawns in the selfish schemes they wish to promote. Sometimes their dislike for a son-in-law or daughter-in-law is taken out on the child. Sometimes parental discipline, or even respect, is undermined through belittling, dishonoring remarks.

Perhaps, however, innuendos, niceties, and shaded meanings are not practiced at all. Certain members of the foursome are designated as friends and others as enemies, and all the world may know. In fact, it sometimes seems that a mother or father feels called upon to be personally responsible to make certain that, indeed, all the world does know. They buttonhole every friend, relative, or passerby to keep the news current.

As with most generalities, there are outstanding exceptions to the trouble-making mother-in-law. I recall a conversation which took place among a group of attorneys while waiting in a judge's chamber. For some reason the talk turned to mothers-in-law, and every one of the five men in the room had a highly complementary statement to make regarding his mother-in-law. In fact, three of them agreed that they felt closer to their in-law-mother than to their natural one. One young man expressed it this way: "My mother-in-law understands me better than my own mother does. I can talk to her about anything, and she will listen. In fact, she is likely to take my side in a disagreement between my wife and me. She's a real buddy and I think the world of her." Another explained that his mother-in-law made his favorite dishes. There is no doubt that a *good* mother-in-law is a source of great joy.

Mothers-in-law have always come in for more criticism, and also more commendation, than have fathers-in-law. It is only natural that this should be so. Generally, mothers have more opportunity for influence, than fathers do, and they are likely to be more loathe to relinquish it, even when the time of maturity has come to their "baby." A mother often has a tendency to make up to her son what she feels is lacking in the wife he has chosen, or to give motherly help and advice to her little girl, even though that little girl has acquired the status of motherhood herself.

It would be neither fair nor accurate, however, to assume that all fathers-in-law exert either no influence at all or if they do, that it is always good. An example comes to mind of a father who could not release his daughter to a man whom he considered undesirable as her husband. The father assumed the role of head of the new household, and did it so effectively that it took only four years for him to completely undermine the rightful position of the husband. So the marriage came to an end. While it may be true that the new husband lacked noticeably in maturity and responsibility, he was certainly bright enough to have learned for himself. He could have done so even more quickly had a wise father-in-law offered the advantage of friendship and example. Instead, this older man openly defied the authority of the young husband in regard to his wife and the two little children who were added to the family.

In describing the problem to me, the husband's voice tightened and he moved uneasily in his chair in an attempt to contain his emotion. At the dentist's suggestion he had told his three-year-old son that he could not have chewing gum, and he asked the grandparents not to bring it. On the next visit, the first move of the grandparent was to hand a full package of gum to the little boy, saying he thought the dentist was foolish. Sweets were given to the children before meals, naps were ignored, no attention whatever was given to the requests of the father regarding the discipline and upbringing of his children. His wife, unfortunately, humored her father and refused to take a firm stand in support of her husband, even when she agreed with him. Her excuse was that she didn't want to hurt her father's feelings. There was, of course, no hope for such a marriage. No two men can rule a household, just as no two women can run one.

Trouble with fathers-in-law, and often mothers-in-law as well, is more likely to come in connection with money than in any other way. Particularly is this true in young marriages. There is a trend now for youngsters to marry before they are financially able to support themselves. Often it is because of the length of time required for an education, and because of the great expense involved in college and postgraduate degrees. The idea of waiting for marriage is given very little credence, and so a way must be found to marry as soon as possible. This, almost surely, will mean that someone's parents are going to foot a big part of the bills until the young fledglings are able to fly alone. I talked recently with a middle-aged couple who are still "helping out," ten years and three granddaughters later.

Parents find themselves almost defenseless against the logic of the argument presented to them by the starry-eyed young couple, obviously in love and eager to begin a new life: "Why should we have to be separated all those years till we are through school, and then even longer till there is a good job and money to live on? We should be together during that time."

There is a basic truth in the argument that it can mean a great deal to a young couple to live together during the

opening years of a new career and shape their future together, rather than waiting till the man's struggle is over, till
the problems are solved, and then have the ready-made plan
handed to the bride. The advantage, however, is lost if there
is too much parental help, because it is the struggle itself
which produces the glue that holds later on when stresses
and strains come.

How many wealthy, successful doctors, engineers, archi-
tects, lawyers, and businessmen there are who, with their
wives, agree that the happiest years of their marriages were
those starvation years when they were so poor that they
depended upon each other for everything. Their poverty
was not the source of their happiness; rather, it was the
knowledge that each was making a tremendously valuable
contribution to the other and that, together, they were in the
process of building a wonderful future. They were headed
in the same direction and each had a share in helping the
other get there. Sadly for many, once success had been
achieved they ceased to need each other and began to lead
widely separated lives until they no longer even share the
same homes. Of those who do, it is done largely as a social
convenience.

At the risk of being dubbed primeval, I must quarrel with
a modern tenet: that a marriage contains a built-in requirement to maintain a certain standard of living and that to
live anywhere short of this standard is to court disgrace. It
appears to matter to no one what sources are employed or
tapped to reach this necessary level: loans, IOU's, even
parents and in-laws. This level is no small potato. A few
years ago a couple, married a dozen or so years, would have
looked with pride upon their accumulated possessions if

they amounted to what the average young couple now expects to *begin* their married life with.

I don't mean to knock luxury and comfort. I've been headed in their direction for some time, but I do wish to point a long, accusing finger directly at the false, weak-kneed idea that in order to amount to anything, in order to hold their heads up, a couple has to start their married life with nice furniture, nice clothes, china, silver, TV—nice everything. And furthermore, if they cannot afford this kind of life, then someone must help. Sacrifice is a word with no meaning at all, or else it means waiting till day after tomorrow for what you really would like to have today.

Is it necessary, then, for parents who are both willing and financially able to extend help to a young couple to withhold their help instead? No, there is a way that needed help can be given and gratefully received. It is so simple that almost no one bothers to do it. It involves a frank, friendly conversation which includes bride, groom, mother-in-law, and father-in-law. If the young people are asking for particular help, they should be clear and candid as to what it is they are seeking and should have sound reasons as to why they feel parental help is necessary. There are occasions where this is the case. If the parents agree to help financially, they should be certain that there is no misunderstanding as to the amount of money involved, the length of time it is to be loaned, and the exact terms of repayment—if they expect to be repaid. Frequently, there is resentment or bitterness because what one person looked upon as a gift, the other intended as a loan. In dealing with in-laws, never try to outguess the other's intentions; you are almost sure to be wrong, particularly if money is involved.

The same format is necessary if the help is being offered voluntarily by the parents-in-law. Most important, the young husband should be told that he is not in any way being relieved of his responsibility for the well-being of the new family unit of which he is the head. The reason for the offer having been extended should be made clear to him so he may know it is not because his wife's parents do not believe he is capable of properly providing for their daughter. Once he gets this notion in his head, it can grow until he will resent even the gifts which are sent to the babies as they arrive.

"I can provide clothes for my own kids. My wife's folks are always sending over something for them to wear, just as if I would let them go naked," a hard-working young truck driver said resentfully. He was a little ashamed of his resentment and had always covered it in the presence of his wife's parents; but without intending to, he took it out later on his wife. His wife had, of course, noticed the connection between her parents' visits and her husband's irritability and was at a loss to understand his dislike for them. It seemed to her that they were doing far more than could be expected of good in-laws and grandparents. His attitude seemed unreasonable to her, and she found herself resenting it. Unconsciously she began aligning herself with her parents as she defended them.

None of these thoughts were expressed, however, and they continued to ferment and widen the gap of misunderstanding between these two young people who loved each other. As they did not talk about it, they began to talk less and less about other things also, and the communication system eventually broke down completely. Each was amazed at the other's lack of understanding of his attitude when the whole problem came to light in counseling sessions. What a difference there would have been if the magic key of conversation had been applied in the beginning. There was love here, though, on the part of everyone involved, and because of this, there was forgiveness. The grandparents even admitted that they could see selfishness in what they had been doing; they had really been indulging themselves by lavishing gifts upon the children.

This is such a common situation that anyone could supply names and make it fit two or three families which they know personally. Some mothers-in-law even spoil themselves to the extent that they choose furniture and give it to their married child. One I know of gave her daughter-in-law so many clothes that, after four years of marriage, she did not have in her closet one single garment which she had chosen for herself. The restricting part about it was that there was nothing at all the matter with the things given to her. They were attractive smart dresses and suits. They fitted well, and she liked most of them.

"I tried to explain it to Dick" she said, "but I know he didn't understand how I felt. He said I had so much more than I would if we had to pay for them ourselves. Since they *were* the right size and I liked them, it seemed pretty silly that I should mind that someone else had picked them out. Everything he said sounded so sensible that all I could say was that, in spite of it all, I wanted to choose my own clothes, at least some of the time. This sounded like something a foolish, spoiled child would say, even to me, and I know Dick thought so. But doggone it, I do. I'd lots rather have less and have the privilege of deciding what I want."

There just isn't room in any marriage for more than one husband and one wife. When someone else, no matter what their motive, begins to usurp privileges and responsibilities of either of those persons, trouble is bound to result. This is not to say that these privileges and responsibilities can never be shared with a third party, or even more. But, it must be done with mutual consent and understanding. When anyone steps into this sacred territory, it should be done upon invitation—and then with fear and trembling—and with an awareness that any word or action could upset the delicate balance between being helper or intruder.

If only some behavioral scientist would invent a testing device! We could call it "In-law Antenna." An interested, well-meaning mother or father-in-law could, when in doubt, send up their antenna and test the atmosphere. So many particles of enjoyment and welcome would be plainly recorded. The same for particles of "please let us live our own lives." Well, till that day, we shall have to search for more and better ways to make use of the means we have available: good sense, open-mindedness, and the gentle art of candid conversation.

8 The Nameplate over the Bedroom Door

The kitchen of a house, while usually a popular spot with the whole household, is generally supposed to be the domain of the wife. Helpers may come and go, more or less frequently, but the chief of the kitchen is Madam Queen.

The husband also has a room in the house which, in a special unspoken way, is more his than other rooms are. In other words, his name could well appear over the bedroom door. Not that he spends any more time there than anyone else, though perhaps he does, but because he is more responsible for what goes on in this particular room. It is, indeed, a room for a bed, but it does seem that it might have a more interesting name, especially since it is shared by husband *and* wife.

I have never understood the term "master bedroom" which is used widely. I am not sure whether it means the bedroom of the master or if it is the master of all other bedrooms. It is generally used to denote the room used by the homeowner, but it is not the kind of name I feel the room deserves. Well, no matter what it is called, the fact is well known and uncontroverted that it is the room which, probably more than any other, influences the course a marriage will take. A man and woman, having given themselves to one another totally in marriage, will find their time together happy and rewarding or frustrating and lonely, depending to a large degree upon how compatibly they share this room.

The making of love is not a new idea to anyone. If you say those words slowly and think about them you will realize they have a very deep meaning. The "making of love" means different things to different people. But, when fully understood, these words mean the actual creation of a beautiful, indefinable emotion called love. The phrase "making of love" implies, quite directly, that there is an action taken which will bring about a particular result. Love can be created, shaped, molded, influenced; love can be made.

The chief of the bedroom is the more responsible person for the aura of this particular room, which is the barometer for the atmosphere of the entire house. If it is cool in the bedroom, it is likely to be cool elsewhere. On the other hand, if the climate of this room is warm and congenial, chances are the same temperature will permeate throughout the remainder of the house. If a storm is brewing, it is here that the first indications are discovered.

When the storm has passed, it is likely to be here that the way back to quiet and calm was found. Here love *is* made. Here one plus one does indeed equal one. Here the gift of oneself is made complete and there is nothing of one not known to the other. Here sleep is shared, the quiet dreaming hours of rest when bodies are unadorned and natural. Here the new day is met together, sourly or sweetly. The most personal things of ones person: clothes, clean and soiled; shoes; the underneath things no one else knows about; these are all a part of this room. This is where a man and woman truly live together. This is where their voices sound quiet and gentle in the darkness, or where hurt comes out silently in tears against the sheet or sometimes in loud, angry statements too searing and hateful to be said in any other place.

There is a king of this room, and he is the husband. Not just accidentally, either. If love can be made, then it follows that it can be made poorly or it can be made well. Here, the quality of the making bears a direct relationship to the quality of the product, just as it does with any other.

Premarital sexual relations have long been a well-known problem in our society, but even more common now is the problem of extramarital sexual relations. Men and women of all ages, of all social strata are involved in this kind of relationship. No attempt will be made here to analyze the reasons for this behavior, but let us just take a level, practical look at it.

Sociological studies are being made and should be, but, for the most part, basic rules of behavior are the same as they have always been. A man or woman, who is solidly centered in a satisfying emotional and physical relationship with a person of the opposite sex which has been solemnized by marriage (and with parenthood) is not likely to carry on an extramarital affair. If the master of the bedroom has earned this title and wears his crown well, neither he nor his partner will invite or accept an extramarital relationship.

The word "chastity" may be as old-fashioned as a Mother Hubbard nightgown, but, like Rembrandt's art or a queen's precious jewels, the rarity makes the possession more priceless and desirable. I am not enough of a Kinsey to want to survey, but it would be interesting to discover whether a minute percentage of those engaged in extramarital activities do so when they have a willing and capable mate at home.

I imagine a good many husbands, and even a few wives, would suggest a little bitterly that these are hardly the proper words to describe their mates. They might add a few more accurate ones, like cold, frigid, disinterested, inadequate. The simple, flat little answers I get when the direct question is asked mean a great deal. Often the answer is, "Oh, I suppose about average." This means, of course, that the person supposes everyone else to be about as bad off as he. Or at least most others are, except for the fortunate few who may have found an unusually sexy wife. There are some of these, and husbands have admitted rather sheepishly that they just can't keep up with them.

Usually though, the husbands' description of how things go in the bedroom will be, "Oh, all right," or a disappointed, "She's cold. Just not interested." These men have, almost unanimously, a surprising opinion of their wives' attitudes. They would deny it. Nevertheless, they seem to feel that a woman has a predetermined, permanent, unalterable disposition toward sex and that it is largely a matter of luck as to what kind they happen to end up with. Every generation or so there is a new push given to the idea that a little premarital experimentation will help to avoid a mistake in this area and to cut down the odds on the gamble.

Yet, these same husbands seem not at all afraid to risk at least two meals a day with a woman who has very little, if any, accomplishment in the art of cooking. They realize that she has not had the opportunity to become skilful in this area, but are confident that with experience and practice she will become accomplished. Many husbands display considerable patience and good humor during the trial-and-error period. Strangely enough, however, very few have transferred this same attitude to the area of sexual maturity, an area which is, hopefully, even more unfamiliar than the culinary department.

How different the results would be if this transfer could be made. How satisfactory a sex partner a wife will make is not, thank heaven, a matter of grab-bag luck. If a husband feels that he has been cheated and got an ice cube when he thought he had a heating pad, he had better quit grumbling about it and look in the mirror at someone who can do something about it. If she is a nice girl, most of what she knows about lovemaking she has learned from him. If she is a loser, it probably is because she has had a poor teacher. What thinking man would marry a girl he would be proud to have for a wife and then expect her to become a Mata Hari overnight? On the other hand, sex is not unnatural, and a tender and compassionate lover can make it appealing and even thrilling to almost any woman.

The wives also get asked the same question. That is, How would they rate their husbands proficiency in the lovemaking department? It is interesting to note that, more often than not, the husband who has complained of a cold wife is rated by her as being a very poor salesman. Some women even report that their husbands are careless about such things as skipping too many baths, stubble chins, and bad breath. Who can blame a woman for not wishing to share her bed with someone who both looks and smells like Hogan's goat? If he were clean shaven, freshly bathed, and pleasant to be near, he might find a much warmer reception.

We all know that one of the best ways to sell a product is to put it in an attractive package. The husband must be the example and lead the way if he wants his wife to have more than a passing interest in the art of lovemaking. He cannot force her, ridicule her, or expect her to be the aggressive one in the beginning. His instincts are keener, and he can teach her what he knows, waking in her gently and patiently, her answering passion. From this point on, they learn together how to be a completely satisfying partner to each other.

Much disappointment and resentment could be spared young husbands if they were told by their fathers that this process is not a quick one, but often takes years. I wish that brides knew this also. Then they wouldn't grow fearful, as they do, that there is something wrong with them because they do not respond sexually to their husbands. Sometimes this even leads them to question their love and to feel a physical repulsion. What is meant to be one of the enrichments of a shared life often becomes, instead, the instrument which divides it.

Most experts agree, and I think rightly so, that sex alone very seldom either makes or breaks a marriage. But, it surely does have a lot to do with the kind of marriage it is. It seems to me it is a good deal like the difference between being rich or poor. One can live either way, but it is a lot nicer to have the advantage of wealth rather than the restrictions of poverty. One can stay alive and exist on the most meager diet, but how much better to enjoy a life which includes a well-balanced, wholesome diet.

In the same way, a marriage made up of a couple who share a bedroom with happy, pleasing intimacy, which is satisfying to both, have put a solid foundation under their lives which will help them stand safe and secure when hard winds come blowing. If, in their lovemaking, they can lose themselves in the gift they are making and truly reach each other, then here at least is one area where they are one. As long as this sharing is possible, there is a way back out of trouble.

With some couples the privilege of sharing the bed is given and withdrawn in much the same way as a child's allowance would be. While it would be stupid of a woman not to be aware of the great price her husband puts on this privilege, still it surely should not be used as a reward for being good or denied as a punishment for being bad. When sex is the stake you play for, you play a dangerous game.

Eleanor, an intelligent, attractive wife of a well-to-do businessman was guilty of two serious errors. She was attracted to a certain man and he to her, so she yielded to the temptation of his attention and eventually spent a night with him. She was the mother of three fine children and the product of fine upbringing herself, and of course, her conscience would not leave her alone.

Months later, to ease her guilt, she confessed her act to her husband. He reacted in a unique but understandable way. "Well," he said, "apparently you weren't getting enough lovemaking at home. He then assured her that she

would never find herself in that predicament again, because
they would have intercourse every night, seven nights a
week, from then on. This they did, whether either of them
felt inclined to or not. It was done in bitterness and resentment and the result was, of course, disastrous. The wife in
desperation finally sought divorce as an escape because the
husband remained absolutely true to his promise. The incident ends well, however, because the couple did truly love
each other and neither was happy with the divorce. A
serious illness of the wife brought them to a point where
they could forgive one another and the family was reunited.

The sexual relationship itself is unlike any other in life
and in marriage. So variable is it with different people that
it is no wonder it brings about so many misunderstandings,
particularly since there is more deception, subterfuge,
and less frank conversation regarding this part of married
life than any other. Many wives carry on a twenty-year
game of pretend so that their husbands will not know how
distasteful this part of their married life is to them. Some
women, and many men, lie awake hours trying to ignore the
depth of their sexual need for the one lying next to them in
the bed. Yet, ironically, it is this very thing—sex, physical
attraction, and desire—which is more responsible than any
other thing for the bringing together of men and women
into the bond of marriage. To some women, it gives a sense
of power over their husbands. It is the means by which they
can influence the pattern of the marriage. For some, it may
well be the only means they have. But, a great many women
endure the act of intercourse silently and methodically because they consider it a wifely duty, much as doing the
laundry or buying the groceries. What a dismal culmination

for the glorious radiance which first tugged at each heart, which drew them together into an embrace, the male and female of them which needed to be fulfilled.

Certainly the blame must be shared, but it is easy to understand the dismay and disappointment of an American girl, who has heard of and read about the fine art of Latin lovers and the great charm of Frenchmen as they woo their women, when she discovers that the American husband tends to do his lovemaking in a very businesslike manner. She can very soon begin to see his approach as purely functional, and she is almost certain to resent it. It will take her a little time, if her mother gave her proper training, to overcome the psychological barrier of regarding sexual activity as something other than naughty. This will happen naturally enough in time. Once she is freed of this barrier, she will come to accept sex as an integral part of her marriage. Whether it is cataloged along with other wifely chores, or whether it is enjoyed as one of the rich rewards of her love, depends very much on the man whose bedroom she shares. The nameplate over the bedroom door should carry a name, and it should be the husband's bright and clear.

9 Mix and Match

There is a law in the field of electricity, which, though understood by few, is known to many. We hear it quoted sagely by both old and young. Unlike many oft-quoted sayings, this one happens to be true, not only in the area of electrical behavior, but in that of social behavior as well. The law referred to is wrapped up in two words: opposites attract.

In electricity, the terms used are negative and positive, that is, two positive poles are not compatible and will not work harmoniously with one another. The same is true of two negative poles. Yet, a remarkable thing happens when a negative and positive pole are placed together in perfect harmony and the current is permitted to flow uninterrupt-edly—and the prescribed functions are performed with ease.

Life holds some unanswerable questions, one of which may well be, Why do certain people marry the ones they do? Fortunately, we don't often have to answer this question for anyone other than ourselves. But a quick glance around the circle of friends and acquaintances which anyone may have will substantiate the premise that the electrical rule applies to people. There are times when like marries like—maybe for money, maybe for security, maybe for spite, or maybe for plain, pure love—but in those marriages, five will get you ten that the success rating is well below top notch.

George and Louise, married fifteen years, lived in a small town, had three fine sons, and in every way had the appearance of a typical, well-established American family. Yet, theirs was one of the most hopeless problems I have seen. There was no cruelty, no unfaithfulness, no dishonesty. George provided a good living and was a dependable father. Louise took better-than-average care of her home, her children, and her husband. Their lives were well-ordered. Both were intelligent, attractive, and well-groomed. There seemed to be absolutely nothing the matter, and in a way this was the problem.

Never have I seen two such identical people. Except for the masculine and feminine difference, they were the same person. Each was quiet, quite self-contained, and reserved. "It gets so quiet that sometimes I feel like walking through the house beating on a pan just to stir up a little noise," Louise said. I expressed surprise that this could be true of any household with three boys in it, but she said that even they were quiet. The two older boys were in activities which kept them out of the house a great deal, and the littlest boy provided the only real relief from the stifling silence. She went on, "I have watched George when we are out with other people and he can talk as much as anyone. In fact, he can be very entertaining, but with me he has nothing to say."

My later interview with George revealed that he shared Louise's feeling of cold emptiness about both their household and their marriage. "Louise can do a wonderful job on a church committee and she joins right in at a bridge party, but she never has anything to say to me. It's about as exciting as living with a department store mannequin." There was a mixture of regret and irritation in his tone. "She accuses me of the same thing, but it takes two to make a conversation." These two expressed the same fear that time was slipping by and they felt a need to be able to lose themselves in it.

Each of these people had the full potential of being an entirely satisfactory husband or wife to someone, but not to each other. While it was true that each had the potential, neither had the ability to draw out the other. Instead, each waited to be drawn out himself. Each expected the other to be the spark, the stimulator, the ball of fire; and while they waited, the silence thickened and became more and more unbearable. To an outsider, it seems too ridiculous that things should happen as they did, but being ridiculous comes pretty easy for most of us. Resentment crept in and kept the quiet atmosphere of the home from being comfortable, then came suspicions that love was dead. How different the story would have been if one of these two had been able to blow his top occasionally, shout and holler a little, or if they could have had a spat and then made up—maybe even leave a dirty shirt right in the middle of the well-ordered living room floor, just for the pure heck of it. Instead, peace reigned supreme.

To someone living in the midst of constant turmoil, this may appear to be the pot of gold at the end of the rainbow, but not to these two. They felt the frustration of dormant emotion waiting to be triggered into response. I can only imagine what George's wonderful qualities would have meant to a snappy-eyed brunette with a sharp wit and a tongue to match. He would have grown ten feet tall trying to master her. A big tease with a fresh grin could have had Louise wrapped around his little finger in a minute—the kind that would call her Lou and whop her on the rear. She would have looked outraged—and five years younger!

I have come across a couple of exceptions and you may too, but they are the necessary exceptions to prove the rule. There are some people who make fortunes without an education, some who gamble everything on the flip of a coin and win, some who even play Russian roulette in order to prove something or other. But this does not mean that the general rule to the contrary is any less applicable. A closer examination of this kind of successful marriage—that is, where there is not a definite personality contrast—will often disclose another interesting fact. Some people, after many years of marriage, tend to become more and more like one of the two of them. Or they may come so near the goal of perfection as to be like a third person, one who is the best of the combination. In some instances, the husband and wife may even begin to resemble one another in their physical appearance as well as in their actions. Neither of them seems to carry the same quotient individually as when in combination with the other. They do truly complement or complete one another. They have actually engaged in a kind of creation of their own and have made of their union a new entity. The two of them have, in the best sense, become one.

It is the most natural thing in the world that a person would be attracted to someone who differs from himself. For example, a timid, rather self-conscious individual will be quite impressed and pleased with one who has a warm, easy, open attitude toward others. On the other hand, the extrovert will appreciate the opportunity for self-expression which he finds with one who is a good listener. Most everyone with any sense of self-evaluation is aware of certain shortcomings in his personality and enjoys a satisfying feeling of completion when he is closely associated with someone who possesses the qualities he lacks. This satisfying feeling, if coupled with a physical attraction, a few compatible chemicals, and a half-dozen unnamed influences, can, if combined in the proper proportions, result in what is called love—then, if all goes well, marriage.

After this, a very ironic thing begins to happen. Each begins to notice that the other has some very odd notions about life, reacts in the strangest of ways at times—in fact, seems quite peculiar and difficult to understand. The new bride, for instance, gets her feelings hurt when she ought not to, according to her husband. Instead of blowing up about it, she turns silent and sulks without even telling him why. Or just the opposite: she blows up over everything, and before he has figured out why she got mad, she is over it and apparently has forgotten all about it. In other words, the differences in temperament are beginning to show up.

Everyone who marries expects a period of adjustment, of getting used to each other. But the big brave smile begins to look a little uncertain when the differences appear. Too many differences, too soon, may become overwhelming, and one or both of the parties may begin to have a sickening feeling of suspicion that they have made an idiotic choice, and that there is no hope for compatibility between the two of them. The very charm of contrast, the "unlikeness" of them, has begun to push them apart, yet this is the magic adhesive to mold them into one.

A fiery little redheaded waitress was tempted many times to throw a plate at her husband when he refused to be drawn into her tirade about something or other. His theory was that it takes two to make a fight, and he knew her well enough to know that in a matter of minutes she would have it all out of her system. It made her madder than ever, though, because when she was mad, she *wanted* to fight. It seemed to her that he ought to get mad enough to fight, too, and that he was completely unfeeling and unresponsive to situations which were very important to her. She had a redheaded humor as quick as her temper, however, and was able to laugh at the picture of how life would be if her husband were to get as mad as she, and as often. "There would be bloodshed for sure," she grinned. "Sometimes I get so mad at him my face gets scorching hot, and I guess it is a good thing he stays calm and cool at those times. If we ever got that mad at each other at the same time, somebody would have to call the police to stop us short of murder." She paused a moment, then added with fire and ginger, "But he looks so piously composed, he makes me think of an iceberg."

The analogy was a fortunate one because, with no prompting from me, the girl was sharp enough to recall the statement she had made a few minutes earlier about her smoldering, scorching anger. She made the sensible conclusion. Just a little abashedly she said, "I guess an iceberg is just exactly what it takes to put out a fire." She was ready then to understand and accept my statement that each of them might be a bit extreme and could benefit by moving a few steps toward more middle ground, but that together they balanced out quite well. She felt ready to be appreciative, rather than resentful, for a husband whose temperament was so different from hers. She was able, also, to see that if she no longer resented this difference, much of her cause for anger would be automatically eliminated.

Did you every hang a door? Probably not, but you may have noticed that there is a little smooth-looking hinge fastened to both the door and the wall. Before the two are put together, they look very odd; each side has little round places which jut out, and there are open spaces in between, all exactly the same size. The corresponding side of the hinge, which is attached directly opposite, looks very much the same, except that the open spaces and the metal loops are in precisely the opposite places so that they slide together and make a single unit. Where each has an opening, the other has a corresponding loop to fill it. When properly in place, a straight metal rod is dropped in from the top so that there is no possible way the parts may become separated, and they function as a single unit. The analogy may seem crude but it is quite apt. It shows quite graphically how two opposites accept each other, each filling the empty places of the other. Each has places of strength and places of weakness. Since they do not overlap but fit into each other, the union of the two is far stronger than either half would be.

I think it is seldom that this view of marriage is taken. Yet, here one plus one does indeed equal one. The two halves, different not only as male and female but in many other ways also, become, when combined, an entity, a whole, the nucleus of a family.

In nearly everything written or said on the subject of marriage, the idea that a good marriage is a fifty-fifty partnership is given another boost. I do not like to find myself in disagreement with so many, but nevertheless that is the case. I have never seen a marriage, successful or otherwise, which was divided down the middle, and I never expect to. And if there ever were one, it wouldn't work, no matter how good the theory sounds. It is like a lot of other notions that sound good on paper but hang high on a limb when the living test is applied. There is no organization which will work on that kind of basis. Ask any businessman you know. There has to be someone with more authority than anyone else, or the whole affair will surely come to a standstill. We will all agree that the marriage relationship differs economically from a business one, but still it is made up of persons banded together in a common effort for a common goal.

It is surely another agreed certainty that sooner or later there will be a disagreement between the parties. What is to happen then? I asked this question of a class of high-school seniors who had stated emphatically that they thought it should be an equal partnership. There was a brief silence as they considered the possibilities, then a girl suggested, "Let them take turns in having the final say in case of an argument." She seemed pleased with the thought, and I imagine it sounded pretty sensible to a naïve, unmarried eighteen-year-old. But you could never sell it to anyone else—not to anyone with more than six weeks' experience in the marriage game anyway. Their question would be the same as mine: Who's going to keep track of turns? That's just something else to argue about. A serious young man in the back of the room suggested that, before the wedding, the couple should decide who would have authority over what problems. I am sure this would work quite nicely with Cinderella and Prince Charming, but it isn't likely to with anyone else. Life, even for single people, is rarely so simple that its problems can be categorized that easily. This is even less likely for married people.

There are some who make broad, general divisions and stick closely to them—like the husband who says, with a certain amount of pride, that he and Mom decided right from the beginning that he would make the living and take care of the outside of the house, while she would take care of the inside and of the kids. He is the same man who wonders why his children do not feel close to him, and why his wife does not seem to need him except when something goes wrong. My comment to him had to be, "In the beginning you asked for only a part of a marriage; that is all you worked at, and that is all you have."

It is hard to imagine how quickly a large slice would be taken off the divorce rate right where it counts the most and rises the highest—that is, in young marriages—if another vow were added to the wedding ceremony. As marriages are not divided evenly, they therefore are unequal, and in every union there is someone who works harder, who cares more, and who gives more. In fact, I have seen some so off balance that, rather than fifty-fifty, they were about ninety-ten. But, if it works for them, who is to say it is wrong?

After all, the one who contributes 90 percent to the marriage gets that much more out of it. The best way, of course, is that neither should have to give disproportionately all the time. The burden should shift from time to time, and each should be ready to assume his share when called upon. Anything is easier to carry if you can put it down occasionally and rest. Otherwise, it seems to grow heavier until it outweighs everything else.

While the "I do's" are being said, just suppose that the bride and the groom were silently making another vow—one between themselves and their God, in which each would say: "In this marriage I will be the one to give the most, to work the hardest. I will be the one who sees to it that this marriage is a happy one. I will be the one to go more than halfway." The making of this promise in the quiet depths of the heart, and the keeping of it, would amount to stamping a golden guarantee of success upon the union. It could not fail.

10 One Plus One Equals One

We are told that the American woman is envied by women the world over, and for many valid reasons. She has opportunities available to her which, in many other countries, are available to only a fortunate few. In America, any girl of average intelligence and financial means can, if she possesses the desire and ambition, choose what she wants to do and where she wants to do it. She has available to her good-looking clothes, a good education, good food, and a good job. She has as much opportunity as though she were a man. In fact, since 1965 she is protected by law from being denied any of these opportunities just because she is female rather than male. She has at last been granted what militant groups of women have fought valiantly to gain; she has equal rights.

To women in less enlightened societies this must seem to be the panacea for all the things they desire: to be removed from the position of servantship in which they are held, to be permitted to have a voice in decisions which affect them, to be free to choose their way of life, to have independence and authority over their person—to have all this and one thing more, equality with men. The drive for freedom was born out of this kind of deprivation and subjection.

The push for equality is a big one these days. Everyone wants it. This must, indeed, seem to be the glittering, price-less goal toward which the young girl's heart yearns when she is denied even the basic right of choosing her life's mate. This still occurs in some parts of our world.

Freedom has come to the American woman in fresh, big gulps, and she has loved the taste of it. It has proved to be a bit addictive, though, and she has not yet satisfied the inher-ent craving which is part her own and part hers by inherit-ance from ancient women. The pearl of great price which she has sought is absolute equality with man—equality not only in *most* areas of her life, but in *all*. Technically, at least, she has obtained her desire. Equality is written into the law of the United States. She must be treated and adjudged by exactly the same standards and rules as if she were a man. She holds the long-sought, yearned-for pur-chase in her hand.

Now that she has bought it, she ought to turn it bottom side up and look at the price tag. It is too late for regret, of course, because the purchase has been made and the con-tract signed. The price tag had not been noticed before.

If a man is hungry enough, he will not quibble over the price of food. A woman might settle for a neat little gingham dress before she feels the expensive smoothness of silk and satin, as it slips over her head and suddenly changes her into a glamorous creature. It is too late, then, to talk about price. But one blue Monday the bill does come and it seems higher than it ought to be. The mere fact that something is expensive does not mean that it is overpriced. This is true only if one pays more for an item than it is worth. It takes arithmetic—addition and subtraction—to arrive at a conclusion. The gains are obvious and, at first glance the cost seems infinitesimal. A good shopper has to beware of hidden costs and learns to prod and poke a little. When this is done, the ledger sheet of feminine equality must carry a debit column as well as one for credit. Can we ask to be treated as men in offices, factories, and stores, but expect to be treated as women when we are off duty? Can we continue to expect the courtesies which have traditionally been extended to women and, at the same time, demand equal treatment with men?

We have drawn neat, orderly lines which carefully mark off the areas where we wish to be treated as men. I think this is asking a bit too much. If we want to be on an absolutely equal footing with men, then we ought to accept the responsibility that equality carries. To be honest, our emancipated woman will have to assume a role entirely different from any she has had yet. She will have to quit jumping out of her trousers, into her skirt, and back again a half-dozen times a day. Instead, she must fold the feminine skirt, put it in a box on the top shelf of the closet, pull the masculine trousers on, and forget her former role.

Someone has come up with a phrase which describes the big push for uninhibited freedom to do anything and everything; it is "unbalanced individualism." Individualism is worth the seeking and is a factor in much success. But when it becomes its own goal, a person is thrown out of balance. Individualism is beneficial, both to the one seeking it and to those in his environment, when it is sought in consideration of others and for the purpose of sharing with them the fruits of the effort. As a nation we are learning that the expense of unbalanced individualism is a threat to national harmony, order, and decorum. Always, one must be aware that his rights extend only as far as encroaching upon the rights of others begins. This principle certainly holds true in society, and equally so in the home.

I am a bit abashed to say so; but, I believe that my sincere, capable sisters have been sucked in and have bought a nice, juicy, political "plum" which has a big worm in it. "Equality" reads well on paper, sounds lovely to the ear, and even looks good on the paycheck. But, there is a hidden cost. It is hidden so well that, even when it starts pinching, we won't be quite able to tell where the hurt is coming from. It will remove injustices which have long existed in pay and opportunities, but will it make better wives? The concept of husband and wife forming a partnership is a long established one, and one with much merit. This ideal, while it may appear only fleetingly and escape mistily just ahead of the grasping, is nevertheless worthy of the effort first to understand and then to create.

Some form of marriage has been found to be present in every society, no matter what the degree of civilization. Marriage, as it is known in the freedom of the Western world follows a pattern which is traced directly from the format set out in the New Testament of the Bible. It is difficult for women born to freedom to realize the tremendous impact that words, now so familiar, made when they were spoken many centuries ago. The statements referred to are found in Paul's letter to the Ephesians and were written to the followers of Christ very shortly after his life on earth: "So ought men to love their wives as their own bodies. He that loveth his wife loveth himself. For no man ever yet hated his own flesh; but nourisheth and cherisheth it, even as the Lord the church: For we are members of his body, of his flesh, and of his bones. For this cause shall a man leave his father and mother, and shall be joined unto his wife, and they two shall be one flesh" (5:28–31). Christian husbands were admonished to love their wives not just a little but completely, and to the same extent that they loved themselves.

The concept of a husband extending love to his wife was quite revolutionary. The common practice was to look upon a woman as a chattel, a very valuable one because she was able to bear his children and in particular sons. If she failed to do this, she was disgraced and another wife was added to the household for this purpose. The Christian format for marriage, as set out in Ephesians, called for one wife rather than many. She was to be treated with love and respect and regarded as a cherished treasure, not as a possession. The ideal of marriage referred to earlier is clearly set out here; it is more than a partnership. It is a union of two who become one. The concept that "they two shall be one flesh" is the basis for this ideal and can be found elsewhere in the Scriptures. A woman was no longer a chattel and valuable only because she could bear children; but, she was an individual with personality and worth and was permitted to share a part of her husband's life now. It is in the New Testament that the "one flesh" principle is found.

The "one flesh" concept of marriage places this relationship in a unique category and separates it from all others.

The acceptance or rejection of this concept determines
whether one is to be found in the ranks of those who hold
sexual intercourse to be a sacred part of married life, or in
the ranks of those who believe it is simply a special method
of giving one's all to life. It is believed by many that, in
God's sight, this union is supremely significant, that the
union of the flesh is that act which consumates the actual
marriage of two people and makes them one. From this
viewpoint, which is well established, the civil ceremony is
simply the means by which a man and woman affirm their
desire and intention to live together as husband and wife, but
an official's pronouncement does not make it so. This does
not become an actuality until the union of the flesh is completed. At this moment the gift of one to the other is offered
and accepted; the two then do truly belong to each other.
To those who buy the "free love" theory, the "one flesh"
concept seems either quaint and peculiar or plain lunacy.
To the free lovers, the total sharing of their bodies is simply
a fine way to show that they care for another; but, the act
carries with it no further responsibilities.

Married or unmarried, however, there can be no such
thing as a casual sex act. Evidence of the unusual significance of the physical union lies in the fact that under both
Mosaic and Christian law, a violation of the union was
considered to be valid basis for divorce. This act necessarily
involves one's total being; and, intended or not, this carries
with it a great significance. There is total involvement; all
the noes have become yeses; the two are one.

Elementary to the understanding of the importance of
this union is an understanding of its real purpose. The male
and female differences did not accidentally occur, nor were

they fashioned as they are solely for the pleasure of humanity. The purpose was, of course, for a continuation of the creative process, the procreation of the human race. This is where the significance lies. The fact that the power of procreation has become a threat due to the uncontrolled indulgence in sexual pleasures does not extinquish its enormous individuality. Medical advances in the field of contraception have removed much of the fear of unintended pregnancies, especially since the advent of "the pill." While this makes a more casual attitude toward promiscuity possible, it does not change the basic purpose or the psychological results of the act.

Through the union of the flesh, more than in any other way, each person gives his entire self to becoming a part of the other one. Marriage, in the Biblical sense, is more than the modern idea of "sharing." It is actually "belonging" to each other, not only physically, but in the subordinating of individual dreams and goals to those which involve the other. The husband without question becomes so much a part of his wife that if he has anything against her it is as if he had something against himself.

There is magc in that idea. It is impossible to view marriage from this standpoint and at the same time accept the modern "equal split" idea. There is competition now between husband and wife that would be inconceivable under the New Testament concept. A man would not compete with himself. Neither would he mistreat, abuse, or neglect his own flesh. By our nature we avoid pain, discomfort, and unpleasantness; this same care and consideration is to be extended to the person of the wife by her husband.

But that phrase "belong to" doesn't appeal one bit to the

American female. She is headed for equality and independence; and, according to her road map, that is in exactly the opposite direction. There is another word she doesn't like any better and this is "submit." That doesn't fit in her vocabulary either. But the word is there anyway, and it wasn't just tossed in to fill up space (cf. Ephesians 5:22–24). Seems to me that if we gals are so smart we should have figured out by now that there is more than one door out of the dilemma. Submission does not necessarily mean the abdication of one's personality and individuality.

The feminine qualities are to be expanded and enhanced, not particularly for the wife, but as an increased benefit for the marriage. This is the important difference. The competitive spirit which exists so commonly between husband and wife today is largely due to this difference in emphasis and motive. It becomes individual rather than mutual; personal rather than marital. A husband, confident that he is revered and respected by his wife will permit her far more freedom in self-expression than one who fears her as a competitor for his authority.

There is a way by which a man can permit his wife to enjoy the benefits of her emancipation and still gain her acceptance of him as head of the family. It may appear to be incongruous, but it is not. A husband does not need to be dictatorial or domineering to prove his authority if he will but permit his wife the American privilege of a personal opinion separate from his, the privilege of disagreement. There is much to be said for the partnership concept of marriage when it is held in perspective. That is: each partner should be given the opportunity for self-expression, knowing that his opinion will be accepted for its worth and will have some consideration in the final decision. That decision will usually be made by the one so authorized, of course, but only after deliberation. A wife who is treated in this manner is not likely to demand more authority or to rebel against suppression.

Lela was a woman of at least average intelligence, average education, and capabilities. She had three children and had given them good care. She had made every attempt to be a good mother and wife, but after seventeen years she finally rebelled against what had come to represent imprisonment to her. She had been given no voice in the handling of the family finances. She had to obtain approval for any activity outside the home. She was, in short, expected to behave very much like an obedient child. Any diversion from this behavior was sure to bring some kind of punishment from her husband, varying from loud vocal belittlement to not too gentle physical roughing up. Milton made certain that Lela knew she was his possession and under his authority and control.

Belonging to one another is not the same as being possessed by another. There was a delightful and healthy change in the atmosphere of the marriage after Milton became aware that Lela was his partner and was capable of making a much greater contribution to the marriage than he was permitting her to do. He had been fearful of giving her any authority, believing that her gain would be his loss. He had drawn the lines tighter and tighter around her, making her more and more rebellious, so that each reacted to the other in an endless circle of resentment. After counseling, Milton relaxed the bonds of her tight little world and permitted her to grow and participate in other areas of life. She

not only became a more worthwhile and fulfilled individual, but a more satisfied and successful wife as well. She had no desire, really, for authority or for personal liberties which were contrary to those of her chosen role of wife and mother. She simply wanted the opportunity to be an individual, not for herself, but as an integral part of a whole.

Well, womankind has her hat on—set straight and pulled down. With a determined look in her eye, she is on her way to the goody shop. But she is still, above all, woman, and this is cause for hope. She is made for man and knows it, and praise God she has a tender place which just can't resist that certain guy. She may have to get her fill of equality with men to find out that this isn't what she really wants. She wants what women have always wanted—opportunity. She wants opportunity to learn, to dream, to do, to go, to be herself—but not *for* herself. She is not a whole but a part, and she is not truly satisfied until the self, which struggled valiantly to become, has lost its heart to another. Hold her, you husband, but hold her loosely, gently, and carefully so that she can be near and far, yet always know that you are there and she is not free.

11 The Crisis and the Counselor

The moment comes when things cannot continue as they are. That moment, set apart from all the rest, when, with sudden clarity, awareness comes that a decision must be made. It is a critical moment. After it, a change has taken place, even before the choice of what to do has been made. A decision to decide is sometimes as important as the conclusion which is eventually reached. Choosing a new path may not be as significant as determining to change from the present one.

That significant moment comes in all areas of life, when suddenly something important has taken place. Illness has been defeated and health begins its return; an adolescent is no longer a child; a flirtation has crystallized into love or annoyance has deepened into hatred. It happens in marriage also. One day the situation, long endured, is suddenly intolerable. Something has to happen. Someone is face to face with a crisis. Once the moment is recognized, accepted and passed, the question narrows. What now?

Understanding the natural progression of changes in attitude and environment would help take some of the pain and anxiety out of that question. These times are almost certain to occur during the course of a marriage. They may, in fact, be expected to return within certain predictable periods. They need not be taken as indication of failure as they often are.

Almost any girl, married from three to five years, will recognize something of the emotion in Jane's voice as she said, "Bob takes me for granted any more. It scares me to look into the future. I sometimes wonder if he is sorry he married me, and I even have doubts about it myself." She sounded frightened, discouraged, and a little angry, all at the same time. The moment had come earlier for Jane than for some, because she had married at nineteen and the babies had arrived so soon.

Might as well batten down the hatches for another trying time somewhere between the tenth and fifteenth year. Roger put it this way. "There's got to be more to life than this. We've been married twelve years and all we've got to show is a bunch of debts. I have just realized I am killing myself for nothing. Something's going to change, or they can just get along on their own." From the way he said it, there was no doubt that he meant to stand by his decision.

And later, one might hope that, having weathered the storms until the silver anniversary time, smooth sailing was guaranteed. It would seem so, but this is not the case. In some ways, the problems of this time are the hardest of all.

Jim and Grace sat in their eighth floor apartment and watched the city lights come on. They seemed content to let the darkness creep through the large picture window and fill the room. Each was silent. A half hour passed. Jim turned on a lamp, muttered something about being gone for awhile and left. Grace, hearing the door close, knew the moment had come for her. She looked around the room, beautifully furnished, filled with mementos of fascinating places and experiences. There were photographs of their children and one of the new twin grandsons. She sat there a long time, as if she were waiting for something to happen. Jim did not come home that night, and early in the morning Grace packed a suitcase and moved to a hotel.

Peace and quiet are generally considered desirable, but silence can be deadly instead of serene. The left-over relationship of a one-time husband and wife can be as cold as yesterday's mashed potatoes. What little conversation there is, is perfunctory and polite. The subjects discussed are rarely more personal than how well one does or does not feel. The couple would do very nicely as brother and sister or possibly distant cousins.

"I am not going to live a lie another day. I have had it. Either I am Jim's wife or I am not, but I am through pretending." Grace told me of the events of the night before, and of the awful hurt she carried inside herself. "I have had it so long that I imagine there is a hollow place somewhere to make room for it." It had started first the time she found a trace of lipstick on one of Jim's handkerchiefs as she sorted the laundry. He had seemed remote and withdrawn and she concluded this was why. She said nothing until several unmistakable smudges later. There had also been a couple of mysterious calls from unknown women and two or three broken appointments with Grace. When she confronted him, he said cutting, hateful things about her being a jealous, suspicious old woman, and to mind her own business. Since that day almost a year ago, they had shared the eighth floor address but little else.

"Last night when Jim went out again, I knew it had to be the last time. Maybe it was because of my cleaning lady that I felt this way." She had asked to leave a little early that afternoon. Grace told of the look of love and the smile as she had explained, "I want to get home as quick as I can. My Ed is feelin' bad and I don't like him to be alone. It means a lot to him to have me there when he's not feelin' good."

First, the moment of deciding that something must be done, then the awesome dilemma of choosing the course to be taken. Grace had come to discuss counseling, not because of any real hope for success, but because it seemed a little less humiliating than divorce. She expressed the opinion early in our conversation that she realized counseling could help early in life, but it was too late for Jim and her. I inquired if I might call Jim and ask him to come in.

He arrived on the agreed day, prompt and friendly. I began my conversation with him making use of an elementary tool of counseling. I attempted to discover what Jim's true desires were; that is, what his highest hopes were, if any, as far as he and Grace were concerned.

"She's the finest woman I've ever known," he said. "She has the qualities I admire; integrity, intelligence, excellent judgment. There was a time when she met every need I had, but that was a long time ago."

One of the nicest experiences I have had was watching these two successful, worthwhile people slowly, almost timidly, build a bridge across which they could eventually reach one another. Jim had first to be given time to decide that he was willing to jeopardize his present situation for the uncertainties of rebuilding with only scraps. He was not prepared to answer my inquiry that first day. Once he concluded that he was willing, however, he began with typical energy and enthusiasm to work and plan toward that end. Later, he reflected that he believed the reconciliation actually began when he fully realized Grace's reasons for seeking help.

He had been wary in the beginning and supposed her real intention was to punish him in some way. He was not entirely free of guilt, of course, and this created a certain amount of reluctance also. There was admiration in his voice, though, as he recalled, "I never thought Grace would do anything about the way we were living."

Grace's reasons for seeking counseling were not unlike those of many others. More and more, this is one of the possible courses to be considered. There is widespread ignorance and misunderstanding, however, about the whys and hows of marriage counseling. Typical reactions to the suggestion are: "No outsider is going to tell me how to live my life." "I don't need anybody to tell me what my problems are, I already know." "You just want someone to agree with you that you are right and I am wrong." Another old favorite is: "We don't really have a problem. If you will just straighten up and do right, everything will be fine."

Some of these statements are sincere declarations and others are frantic blockades set up as protection against the painful experience of coming face to face with a marriage counselor. This is an experience looked upon with actual fear by some, with open antagonism and resentment by others, and tolerant disdain by a good many spouses who have been pressured into coming. It is refreshing to see these attitudes give way, slowly to be sure, as the counselee begins to understand what is expected of him. It is a rare human being who will not react favorably to a situation in which he learns that he is free to be himself. He is given, in the counselor's office, an opportunity to express himself without danger of recrimination and with certainty of being heard.

It is my belief that the counselee deserves not only to be listened to but also to be answered. I have never been in agreement with the school of thought which held that the role of a counselor was to be a listening post and little else. An ordinary wooden fence post would do as well, and would require considerably less money and inconvenience. Fortunately, there is now a widespread and rapidly growing acceptance of directive approach and a corresponding rejection of the non-directive approach to counseling. This change has come about largely because of the most powerful evidence of all, success. The trial and error method may be the long and painful method of determining facts, but it is also the most incontrovertible.

Experience has taught those who are willing to learn that people respond more fully and more quickly when there is an exchange of ideas. The most effective counseling session is one which includes dialogue. The counselor may want to avoid the use of direct questions, but information can be obtained and suggestions can be made in many ways. In fact, it would seem to border on professional irresponsibility for a counselor to be aware of a sound solution to a client's dilemma and still sit silently through months of conferences, waiting for some distant day when the client might possibly come up with the thought himself. Happily, this silent listener is being replaced by one who offers much more. This change has been slow in coming, but it has a very widespread influence. The deep psychotherapy which has for years been thought to be helpful in solving marital problems is now being questioned also.

Does counseling always help? Are there ever times when it is useless?

If a husband and wife each agree that they no longer wish to continue their marriage, then there is no service which a counselor can provide. If, however, either of the parties wishes the marriage to continue and the other is reluctant, it would appear that some productive time could be spent. The question of why the relationship was satisfactory to one partner and not to the other requires an answer, not a superficial one but one which has been reached after facing all the possibilities of change. If a husband and wife both wish the marriage to continue, if both also agree that the relationship is not a satisfying one as it presently exists, and if both further agree to cooperate, then success is within their reach.

The counselor does not, of course, solve people's problems for them. His purpose is to help them come to a better understanding of themselves and of the one to whom they are married. Interesting discoveries are made in interviews in which both partners participate. What each expects of the other and of the marriage may be very similar, or the expectations may differ widely. This is vital information, because if two people are headed in opposite directions it is not likely they will arrive at the same destination. A skillful counselor will not only discover this but will also guide the two toward an even more important answer. Is either willing to change his goal so that it will more nearly conform to that of the other?

Sometimes it is necessary to involve the children of the couple if they are an integral part of the difficulty. Many marriages are so child oriented that all decision making requires approval from the children before it is acceptable to the adults. An extreme instance of this resulted in a severe case of ulcers for an eight year old boy. He was given too much responsibility and too little guidance by parents who thought they were doing him a favor.

The concept of group counseling, or group therapy, is gaining much popularity because of the same dependable measurement, results. This technique is used, not only for a family group, but for unassociated people as well. This method is growing rapidly in acceptance and use, not only because of its effectiveness, but also because it is a way of caring for a larger number of people in a designated period of time. Counselors are so few, and critical situations are so abundant. Participation in therapy of this kind often brings about response to others' attitudes and actions which is not attainable in individual counseling. The inter-action of emotions and ideas has great value in helping one to determine and establish his own concepts. One also becomes less self-concerned and self-involved as he becomes more involved and concerned with others who have needs. Agony over self can be expected if the view of life is always turned inward.

Remember George? With nothing but debts and ingratitude? It certainly seemed so to him as he pulled into the driveway after working late, as usual. Everyone had gone to bed, and he sat in the car and looked at the darkened house. It was here that he reached the decision he had later related to me. "I never knew it was possible to feel as alone as I did that night, or as tired, either. I thought about Fran and the kids asleep inside the house and I knew that all I was to them was a dollar sign."

There was a reason.

Five years ago George had taken a big gamble. He had mortgaged everything, including the house, and borrowed heavily in order to build a new printing plant. He knew it would mean sacrifice for years to come, but the old equipment just wasn't up to the job anymore. He cut every corner possible, including personnel, and had taken another's job in addition to his own, but it had been worse than he had expected. He had worked harder and longer, and had, of course, less and less time with the family. His contacts with the children were so limited that there was never time for relaxed conversation and exchange of happenings. He had lost touch with their activities and projects. It just seemed to him that they were always coming and going, always needing something, and he could not remember seeing the results of anything. They seemed always out of lunch money, and in need of two dollars for allowance or ten for shoes.

He just didn't understand Fran at all. She was so different from the woman she used to be that she might as well be a stranger. She seemed to have no interest in the plant, and he seldom mentioned what happened there. Their lives had become more and more separated, so that now there was almost no intimate contact. He used to, on occasion, attempt a gesture or expression of love, but nothing ever came of it. He was not quite sure if it had been misunderstood or ignored. Either way, he let it go.

George had gone into the house that night, had wakened Fran and told her of his decision. He was too weary to quarrel, and she did not get an answer when she sleepily asked him what in the world he was talking about.

Fatigue was one of the big factors in the development of George's crisis. He was very near the point of exhaustion physically, and his emotional health was little better. He had isolated himself so completely that his point of view was badly warped. It was he who saw life only in its relation to money and to himself, and neither aspect seemed to be making any progress. His astonishment was obvious when, in my office, he heard Fran describe her abandonment. The plant had come to be an enemy because it had destroyed their home. She felt completely shut out of George's life and believed he worked late by choice much of the time. He had not shared his concern and worry with her, and she was unaware of how much he was demanding of himself. During that interview George, for the first time in many months, began to see life as it affected others and to get a view of himself as he appeared to someone else.

This was a breakthrough which resulted in a quick, practical solution. Fran, after so much confinement with the children, eagerly agreed with the suggestion. She began going to the plant three afternoons a week to post the checks and keep the books. This relieved George of much of his night work, as he had been doing it himself to avoid expense. There was an added benefit also. Fran developed a new understanding of the real financial structure of their business. Her perspective was a much more enlightened one as she had actual contact with the credits and debits. She no longer resented the time and energy George put into the work there but, instead, felt a part of it. The free evenings at home made it possible to reestablish a family life so that George was able to be a participating parent.

It is not true that all situations are so easily corrected, or that there are never any which fail to respond. It is true that the behavior of some people is so extreme and irresponsible that it becomes impossible for a marriage to continue. This conclusion should not be reached until all possibilities have been explored and until there has been a recognition of the new problems which divorce may present.

A realistic look at married life points unmistakably to the fact that nothing is without change. Life is, it seems, a continuous adjustment. There are "stages" in the development of a marriage just as in the development and growth of a child; and, it would seem, with almost the same accompanying problems. There are healthy, ongoing marriages, however, which exist today because a crisis which came to those involved was viewed not as a failure but as a challenge.

12 How Firm a Foundation

A little incident which changed a man's life was related by him to his minister. The story contains a great lesson, hidden as many great things are, in ordinary, everyday circumstances.

The day after Christmas Mr. Greene parked his new car in front of the local drugstore to run in and pick up a morning newspaper. As he pulled to a stop, he noticed a dirty, poorly dressed boy standing in front of the store, watching him with a great deal of interest. Mr. Greene recalled thinking to himself that he had better hurry in and get back to his car as soon as he could, or he might be missing a hubcap or two. The way the youngster was eyeing his car made him suspicious. He came out of the store with his paper and just as he opened the door of his car to get in, the boy walked over to him and said, "That sure is a beautiful car."

"Mister, how much would a new car like that cost?"

"Well, I don't actually know," Mr. Greene said. "You see, my brother gave me this car as a gift."

The ragged little boy looked unbelievingly from the shiny automobile to Mr. Greene, then back again. Then with a look of wonder in his eyes, he said slowly, "Gee, I wish I could be a brother like that."

It was the next day when the older man called at his pastor's study, but he was still shaken and a little mystified by what the boy had said. "I was so sure he was going to say, 'I wish I could have a brother like that,' but he didn't. He said, 'I wish I could *be* a brother like that.' I learned something from that young boy in that moment that I had not learned in more than fifty years. He showed me what true unselfish love is like." Incidentally, the other part of the story had a happy ending, too. Mr. Greene asked the youngster to get in the car if he would like to, and he would take him home. There he met the little crippled brother and took him for a ride which delighted them all.

Unlike Mr. Greene, many people are not privileged to see a clear-cut profile of undiluted, self-giving love. This kind of love is pure gold; this kind of love lasts and lasts because it does not require that certain conditions be met before it is offered. This kind of love is divine, and this is why it lasts. It is not something cooked up in someone's heart to be dealt out in certain quantities in direct ratio to what is received by him. How pitiful it is to see human beings striving to manufacture within themselves enough emotion called love to last over the long, rough haul of many years of marriage—enough understanding, enough mercy, enough forgiveness. Of course they run out, and, that is when I hear the statement, "I just don't feel anything. I don't even hate him. Sometimes I wish I could. It would be easier than this nothingness that I feel. All I know is, I feel no love for him at all." And it is very true. The hurts have come again in the same tender places until a protective scar has built up and now nothing can penetrate.

In building up protection against pain, often without intending to, one is at the same time immunized against joy. But this is not necessary. The divine kind of love the ragged little boy knew was scarcely related to other feelings which bear the name—self-designed, watered-down facsimiles of love. It is as far removed as the fresh, clear sea breeze is from the smog-thickened, carbonized city fumes. It works in a perfectly marvelous way, really, when used as it was intended.

Way back in kindergarten days, most of us learned in our church or synagogue a brief verse from the Bible which holds a most valuable bit of wisdom. The verse contains three important words, "God is love," and when properly understood, they provide a magic key which will unlock doors that can be opened in no other way. They provide the answer to the heartbroken cry of "How can I go on? Oh, what can I do?" The cry comes when there just is no more feeling, no more desire to forgive, to care, and to try, yet the need persists.

The important thing about the verse is that what it does not say is almost as significant as what it says. It does not say God has love, or that he gives it, or that he knows about it, but that he *is* love. This means that more important than just to know about God, or to be more or less acquainted with him, is the necessity to *have* him in order to have love. There is a basic rule of law that one cannot give away that which he does not own. This is true of possessions, also of love. If God is the source of love, then to know him is to

know love, to have him is to have love. Then, it is no longer
necessary to rely upon oneself for an endless supply of love
to keep the heart tender year after year. Instead, the bound-
less resources of God are made available.

It is much like shifting into overdrive and letting a super
engine assume the load. It is a beautiful thing to see how
smoothly and efficiently God does just that with the very
load which had required such struggling and striving before. When one is filled to overflowing with the love of God,
it is easy to share it, to give it freely to another, because it
does not come *from* oneself, only *through* one, as through a
channel, and the supply is endless.

You say, "But, that is a different kind of love, that's not
the man-woman kind." I disagree. Love is love. There are
just many different ways of expressing it and countless
degrees of it, but the emotion of caring is the common
denominator. We care about everyone to some degree or
other, for some with a slightly more personal feeling which
we think requires an overt action, such as gifts or occasional
calls. For others, such as our parents and grandparents, we
have a feeling of deep gratitude in return for their caring for
us. The joys and sorrows shared by brothers and sisters
certainly create a common bond which binds them to one
another. There is a deep river of affection which flows to the
offspring of one's body, and there is the total giving away of
the heart, the desire to become a living part of another
human being. Each of these relationships is an expression of
love.

The empty heart which can no longer produce love is
likely to produce instead doubts and fears which are expressed tonelessly: "I don't know why I did it." This is the

answer I often hear in response to such questions as, Why were you unfaithful to your wife? Why do you gamble with money your children need? Why do you flirt with other men when you know your husband is angered by it? Very often people in trouble, because of some action they are responsible for, seem at a loss as to why they behaved as they did. If I pursue the question further, the next statement is quite likely to be: "I'm afraid I don't understand myself very well. I do a lot of things I wish I didn't do. As a matter of fact, I really don't like myself much."

How ironic it is! Here the person is presenting himself to another person and in effect is saying, "Here I am, love me. I can't stand myself, but you love me." Here is a neurotic, unbalanced, emotionally lopsided individual who is trying to find someone else to do for him what he needs to do for himself. It doesn't take a psychiatrist to figure out that the only way two such people could find completion in marriage would be if their neuroses happened to fit. Small wonder that there are so many disillusioned people standing in line at the pill counters.

How much better the chances for happiness would be if two people could present themselves to each other as emotionally sound, well-rounded personalities, saying in essence, "Here I am, love me. I'm not perfect, but I'm working at it. You will enjoy me, I know you will, because I am an enjoyable person." This is not at all the same thing as overrated egotism. It is, instead, an acceptance of oneself as a very remarkable kind of creature having a personal relationship with his Creator who permits him to have a certain degree of responsibility in the continuing creative process of his own personality. Such an individual is equipped to offer a great deal to a marriage if his purpose in entering into it is not self-seeking but self-giving. There is a great deal of difference. The difference is so basic that it determines the kind of foundation upon which the entire marriage will rest.

The subject of religion is faced by everyone sometime in life. It is a subject which should be discussed thoroughly by every couple before marriage. If possible, a decision should be reached which is agreeable to them both. How sad and how late are the words, "I thought after we were married everything would work out all right." If only those words, "I now pronounce you husband and wife," contained just half the magical powers that are expected of them, there would be very few problems left to solve.

It is easy to understand why this business of religion becomes involved as frequently as it does and to such a deep extent. It is as personal as the inside of one's mind, and yet it is something which is to become a part of another's thinking. The problem is increased considerably by the fact that many people marry before they have come to a definite conclusion about their personal religious convictions. Ought they to seek help from someone in an equal state of indecision, or from someone with definite opinions, or, just hope that a conflict doesn't develop later on? Suppose a young man has come face to face with the question of what his relationship with God should be and has found what is for him a satisfactory answer. To limit his choice of a bride to one who shares his convictions might seem to narrow the field to a painful degree, but, this could be the most important limitation he could impose. To be practical, the ideas of two persons need not be identical at all. Yet the more similar they are, the greater the value they may be to the marriage. One's acquaintance with God, or his refusal to know him, should certainly rate as high on the evaluation chart as the person's education, his income, or his innate intelligence.

There are statistics, I am sure, to prove the greater percentage of success for marriages of a similar religious faith over those with a dissimilar faith, or for those with none at all. But I do not refer to them. Not that I consider them unimportant, but just unnecessary. There is no substitute for experience; it is what we call the best evidence. The experience of my practice has been that there is a tremendous value in seeking a marriage partner who has a definite religious opinion which concurs with that of the other. Furthermore, this value is immeasurably increased if that opinion is one of a vital, actual faith in God as an integral part of life. There are two particular experiences in marriage which, I believe, do more to bind a man and woman together as a unit than any other. I do not mean this statement to be sacrilegious in any way, but these two experiences, the worship of God and the participation in sexual intercourse, involve the total giving of oneself. The basic reason is the same. In each situation both persons are involved in an experience in which they are lifted out of themselves and become a part of something which is greater than they are individually. When a man and a woman sit or kneel together and join in the common humbling of themselves before their God, there is a bond which binds them to each other in a truly marvelous way. Each is a part of a relationship which unites them into a oneness with God. It is an exciting and stabilizing experience, and it adds a strength to the union which carries over into other areas.

The strength which comes to a couple by means of this experience is important, not only because it expands the boundaries of life, but also because it can be called upon to help when trouble comes in a completely unrelated way. In addition to adding depth to the reservoir of personal stability, there is the extra benefit that the couple can face their problems together on the basis of this relationship. Ideally, they can even join in seeking a prayerful solution.

The belief that divine help is available for solving human difficulties often means the difference between hope and desolation. The marriage of two people who share this belief and who join in a worship experience have a union which rests solidly upon an enduring foundation. There is a unity which is lacking if there is a basic difference in faith —such as Protestant and Catholic, or where one member has no faith at all. There is purpose and power in the union of mutual faith. It holds a husband and wife close during a crisis which, otherwise, would almost certainly cause a shattering trauma.

There is much talk about tolerance of other religions and a great fear of being considered anything less than broad-minded on the subject of religion. I have no quarrel with the philosophy as long as it does not extend to a marriage. There it fits awkwardly, if at all. The possible exception might be a situation in which neither party holds a deep conviction of any kind. This would avoid any conflict in the matter. It would also rob the marriage of an entire strata of living. The enriching depths of perspective would be absent, with a resulting shallow concept of human life.

Philip Gilliam, juvenile judge of Denver, Colorado, and recent president of the National Council of Juvenile Judges makes a flat statement in this regard. "The person who does not hold the religious concept of human life does not know and cannot understand the meaning of life." The kind of religious view held has as much to do with the molding of personality as the kind of education, the means of livelihood, and family background. Yet the modern teaching is that we ought not to judge one on this basis. One is considered extremely narrow if he lets the subject even be a matter for consideration in his evaluation of a candidate for political office. I believe that no person can be adjudged fairly if this matter is not given the utmost consideration, because this is the most accurate barometer of his character.

The individual who sees life as the answer to itself, who sees his role in it as finding fulfilment for himself, and who believes only in known and provable facts, will hold a lesser value of life and will have a corresponding appreciation for human love. A marriage composed of two people with these beliefs is going to be of one particular kind. On the other hand, if a person believes that man has a spiritual nature which can have a personal relationship with a divine Creator, that human life is the extension of that Creator and, therefore, is endowed with the ability to communicate with, and even contain, a spiritual power, then he will hold a far different view of the purpose and value of human life. I have found that he will also have a very different understanding of love.

This poor, beat-up, bruised, and beautiful little word is hooked onto a lot of emotions to which it isn't even a distant cousin. It is handy because it can add a certain amount of dignity to undignified skulduggery—like personal gratification, the need of one person to possess another, physical desire, even convenience. Love is a different thing from self-seeking. Love seeks to *make* happiness rather than to find it. Love that is pure and true has qualities which are more than human—qualities of mercy and forgiveness. On a strictly human basis, these characteristics are available but in ratio to actions of the one to whom they are intended. The kind of love which lasts and lasts, which is not based on what others would do, which extends beyond the reasonable—this is the kind of love which contains a spark of the divine.

To be capable of this kind of love, it is necessary that there is contact with the eternal, changeless love of God. In other words, this kind of person brings an added quality to a marriage, an added potential for riding with the punches, an additional resilience, a greater dexterity in finding solid footing along slippery paths ahead. The heart that holds the love of God is acquainted with, and aware of, love from an altogether different perspective than is a heart capable of producing only human love.

It is comparable to the kind of appreciation shown for a painting by a great artist who is aware of the true art of shading, of form and color. His appreciation of the worth of the work will be far greater than that of one completely untrained and unaware of these values. All that person would know is whether or not he is pleased by the work. His judgment is based solely on a physical response of pleasure or displeasure. How different is the meaning of beautiful music to a trained musician as compared to one who knows nothing of the disciplined study, or of the determined efforts made in the practice room. Nor can he know the great reward and joy of complete abandonment and identification with the music. Dr. Elton Trueblood, author and professor, known throughout the United States as Mr. Quaker, uses the descriptive term "tough love" to describe the Christian characteristic. It is tough enough to withstand differences of opinion without being offended, tough enough to bounce back, not just once, but again and again. Yet tender, too. This kind of love is a letting love, not a possessing love; it holds the loved one, the adored one, tenderly and freely, not with rigid tightness.

It is said there are many kinds of love: brotherly love, passionate love, platonic love, parental love—on and on, with endless differentiations of each. I cannot agree. There is love. Love is a particular emotion, different from any other. It is always what it is, just directed in varying degrees toward different persons. We may permit ourselves to feel wee stirrings and flutterings of it, or we may give our entire selves over to this particular emotion, letting it be the motivation for all our actions. It can be shut off from all humanity with the exception of one or two people, or it can be extended to include the entire human race. It may be given only to those who conform to a predescribed pattern of behavior and appearance, or it can be withheld from all who differ from that pattern.

Married love is different? Only in that it is a way of expressing a greater quantity of love toward one person than to all the rest of the world. One need not run out of love unless he is trying to be the source of his own love. Then, he is dealing in a dwindling commodity. It is imperative for him to have contact with the true source, in order to be certain that he is handling the real product and not a homemade imitation. If it is, it will last for all of life, and the added years will bring quiet wealth of joy.

For Further Reading

DRAKEFORD, JOHN W. *The Home: Laboratory of Life.* Nashville: Broadman Press, 1965.

EDENS, DAVID AND VIRGINIA. *Making the Most of Family Worship.* Nashville: Broadman Press, 1968.

EDENS, DAVID AND VIRGINIA. *Why God Gave Children Parents.* Nashville: Broadman Press, 1966.

HERRING, REUBEN. *Two Shall Be One.* Nashville: Broadman Press, 1964.

HUDSON, R. LOFTON. *Home Is the Place.* Nashville: Broadman Press, 1967.

Arvin, Kay k.

1+1=1.